gather

DAVID
ROBERTSON

gather

A DIRTY APRON COOKBOOK

Figure.1

Vancouver / Berkeley

To our parents, Maureen and Vernon Robertson and Tom and Monika Reimer, who taught us about the love and generosity that happens when we gather around the table.

In loving memory of Monica Nair.

Recipes are chef tested.

19 20 21 22 23 5 4 3 2 1

Cataloguing data is available from Library and Archives Canada
ISBN 978-1-77327-067-8 (hbk.)

Design by Jessica Sullivan
Photography by Kevin Clark
Prop styling by Jessica Sullivan/Naomi MacDougall

Writing by Kerry Gold
Editing by Michelle Meade
Copy editing by Pam Robertson
Proofreading by Lucy Kenward
Indexing by Iva Cheung

Printed and bound in China by C&C Offset Printing Co., Ltd.
Distributed internationally by Publishers Group West

Figure 1 Publishing Inc.
Vancouver BC Canada
www.figure1publishing.com

contents

foreword

Cooking is one of the most of important skills you can learn. Wait a minute, who am I kidding—it's *the* most important. To us chefs, cooking is everything. Whether we're preparing a favourite breakfast smoothie, a simple salad or the most complicated terrine, we are constantly thinking and talking about food. And with so much inspiration to be drawn from other cultures and food traditions, cooking is a never-ending exploration.

Consider the sheer range of ingredients and products. Quality fruits, vegetables and artisanal products can be sourced at local farmers' markets; organic meats at reliable butcher shops; and sustainable fish from trusted fishmongers. We're even seeing a resurgence of wild foods and uncultivated ingredients. In fact, Dave and I both enjoy fishing, foraging and feasting—there simply isn't a better feeling than learning how to catch wild salmon, or discovering a patch of watercress or pine mushrooms. And I promise you, wild food tastes better.

I have so many memories when it comes to cooking personally and professionally. One of my favourites is preparing fresh gnocchi with tomato sauce for the first time. The meal wasn't perfect, but I had made it myself and any imperfections I might see now did not matter then. The experience taught me that cooking is all about planning, which outweighed any intended result.

People often ask me how to make a dish. For learning techniques and how to assemble ingredients, I cannot say enough about The Dirty Apron Cooking School. My son has taken several courses there, and each time he comes home with ideas and questions about all things culinary. He has also learned that part of the fun in cooking is making new food discoveries and building friendships at the same time. You can acquire skills and be inspired in Dave's classes, and with this book, you can create the school's most popular dishes at home.

Gather proves that cooking doesn't need to be complicated; you can cook dinner *and* enjoy time with your friends. Simplicity is the key and Dave and his team have nailed it.

I don't advise trying a recipe for the first time thirty minutes before your guests arrive. It's important to feel comfortable with a recipe, and practice makes perfect. So get reading, and be prepared for a culinary adventure. I hope you find joy in your kitchen, foraging in your backyard and sharing with friends, neighbours and family, as much as we do.

David Hawksworth

introduction

In every aspect of my life—whether it's as a chef, the head of The Dirty Apron Cooking School, a volunteer in my community or even as a family man—food is at the centre of everything I do. In my twenty-plus years as a chef, I've seen food bring people together around dinner tables and classrooms and campfires. I've seen food bring joy and connection; I've seen it enrich lives and forge friendships. I've seen food break down barriers between people from vastly different cultures and backgrounds. Food that is cooked with love and passion is one of life's most powerful unifiers, and it's the reason why I became a chef, restaurateur and cooking instructor. There's a thrill to seeing people get stoked at the realization that they can make their own fresh burrata cheese or panna cotta. That social connection around food is why years ago we started a couples' cooking class at the Dirty Apron, and why we run the popular Kids & Teens Summer Camps. Couples get to know each other better over the creation of food. At the five-day camps, kids learn about the importance of fresh, local ingredients and the process of cooking, from *mise en place* to plating.

But my passion for food isn't confined to my work at The Dirty Apron Cooking School. I learned early on that food transcends wealth or pretention, and I think that goes back to the fact that my dad was a butcher and my mom a devoted home cook. I grew up in a household where we understood the meaning of cooking on a budget, and my mom knew how to

transform an inexpensive cut of meat into something that fell off the bone. The Crock-Pot was always on the go, cooking was usually long and slow—and, believe me, nothing went to waste. And that appreciation of good food, time spent in the home kitchen and gathering people around a table has extended into my own life. Breakfast is a solid family affair at our house, and I get seriously blissed out at the aroma of coffee on the stove, the smell of brown sugar bacon in the frying pan and, most importantly, the connection I have with my kids when they've got their tiny hands in a bowl of biscuit dough, mixing in that cold butter. I hope that one day when they're grown up, they'll look back on these moments in the kitchen and feel the way I did as a kid helping my mom cook.

Food brings us together in different ways, too. I have worked, volunteered and shared food in some places—such as Belfast and Jerusalem—where people had long-standing differences. But the things that we have in common are what unite us. While I was in Israel, I spent time with passionate foodies, and it didn't matter whether they were Jewish or Muslim: we ate wicked bread together and enjoyed highly addictive cookies and confections such as halva, made from a rich sesame paste known as tahini. While I was there, we didn't discuss the strife that you see all the time in the news. We discussed how to make a great loaf of bread.

But you don't have to travel halfway around the world to discover how food unites us. Vancouver may be known for its pristine beaches and majestic mountains, but we have inner city concerns here too, like

any other big city. At the Dirty Apron, we run the Dream Big mentorship program for inner city elementary school kids, taking them on monthly field trips and opening them up to a world of possibility through food. We use food and cooking to bring the kids together, to educate them and to inspire them to make informed choices. The kitchen requires teamwork, and that is such a great lesson for kids. It builds confidence, too. I've seen kids blossom before my eyes when they pull off a perfect rib-eye steak. It's a program that operates in partnership with a lot of great local businesses, and it's become such an integral part of our mission that we're expanding it to include more kids. As a chef with kids of my own, it's the best way I know of giving back to the community.

Our first book, *The Dirty Apron Cookbook*, was about bringing our cooking school into your kitchen, teaching you how to prepare meals like a pro, but without having to spend hours learning techniques. We taught you the importance of brining, how to make stock and how to roll fresh pasta. This time out, we're getting outside the classroom and to the heart of cooking, and why we do it—which is, really, for the people in our lives and for the simple pleasure that is cooking food. These are meals to be shared, on platters and in big bowls, heaped high, served with care, generosity and a lot of love. After all, cooking itself has become more social by nature. Growing up, the cook (a.k.a. mom) was lonely in the kitchen while everyone else watched TV. Now, friends sidle up to the counter with a glass of wine and get chopping. Nobody is banished to cooking duty. It's a collective joy.

We're also including more options for plant-based and gluten-free diets, with our usual Dirty Apron approach: rustic yet sophisticated, classic with a twist—and always delicious.

It's my hope that when you're gathering your own friends and family around the table, you get as excited about the process as I do. Stress has no place at a great meal. To that end, I've put together delicious, crowd-pleasing recipes that are super approachable and easy to prepare, with an emphasis on dishes from around the world (I always pay homage to my travels). Of course, you'll also learn a few techniques along the way, whether it's grilling, braising, roasting, poaching or searing—good cooking is all about coaxing flavours out of your ingredients, and if you get the techniques down, you'll have success in the kitchen and see big

smiles around the table. The kids will go quiet and ask for seconds.

By the way, you don't need to be indoors to make great food with top-notch ingredients. We live on the West Coast, and my friends and family members are outdoorsy people, which means we like our camping, our tailgate parties (for football fans) and our barbecues. All you need is an inexpensive Hibachi and a group of friends at the beach, and you have yourself a party. However, the key to a great barbecue feast lies in the preparation—I've been known to spend two days preparing for a camp-out. I'm the guy at the campground who sets up a home-away kitchen with a prep station and multiple burners, containers of prepped food (outdoor *mise en place*), a cooler of marinated meats, farm fresh eggs, a jug of good olive oil, multiple pepper mills and a bag of fleur de sel. I always have enough to feed a crowd, and nothing goes to waste. I'm in my element, cooking from my barbecue station, with family and friends and excited kids running around. If it's a tailgate party, I'm always wearing a football jersey.

This book features tried-and-true dishes such as the lamb loin (p. 148) and Korean barbecue ribs (p. 142), with my usual twist on flavour. But I'll also nudge you a little outside your comfort zone, with a seared venison loin with white bean–truffle ragout (p. 154) or a salt-crusted whole sea bream with an almond and caper brown butter sauce (p. 108) that comes out of my French classical training. We often look to French techniques because they're timeless and all about pulling those flavours. But I'd like to push you into your creative place, too. Infuse roasted cauliflower with za'atar (p. 65) for one of my favourite soups. Instead of basic oil and vinegar dressing, try tahini-soy dressing on broccolini and snap peas (p. 43) for a change. The soups and salads here are big on flavour, easy to whip up and perfect for gatherings.

We've included a lengthy section on vegetarian dishes this time out—but make no mistake, plant-based dishes can be just as hearty and flavourful as any of our meat and seafood dishes. Many of these are comforting big bowl dishes, whether it be the creamy ricotta gnudi elevated with crispy fried basil (p. 93) or the kale and zucchini spaetzle tossed with toasty pumpkin seeds (p. 82).

The desserts are equally unpretentious and big on flavour, made rich and decadent with a little of the unexpected, like olive oil or avocado. Pastry chef Kat will give you the lowdown on some of her techniques, too, including tips on how to bake gluten-free (p. 188). Her salted caramels (p. 180) are a mainstay at our deli counter, and she's generously shared her recipe here. Make up a batch and drop them into her caramel macchiato cookies (p. 177). And then share them with your friends and family, just because.

Remember, food sustains us in more ways than we might know. It's my sincere wish that this book makes for some of your happiest memories around your dining table, picnic table and campfire. After all, at the centre of this type of merriment is good, honest, food.

mise en place

Mise en place is a French culinary term that means everything in its place, and whether cooking indoors or outdoors, the basics should always be nearby. Good cooking starts with assembling the right ingredients. Begin each recipe by ensuring that you've got good-quality ingredients that are fresh, prepared and measured out. Throw out spices or nuts that have sat on the shelf or in the refrigerator too long, or baking soda that might have lost its leavening ability. A stale ingredient can ruin a dish. Fresh is best.

In my home kitchen, I have all the cooking basics within easy reach, but I also have my personal favourites always in stock, which I'm happy to share:

bacon jam
For the meat lover, a snack doesn't get much better than a big spoonful of bacon jam on a slice of baguette. You can make your own in about twenty minutes, with bacon, sautéed onions, vinegar, sugar and spices. Keep it in a sealed mason jar. It's good for garnishing burgers, too. Bacon jam is available at the Dirty Apron.

bread
It's a rare day you'd enter my home kitchen without finding a big, fresh loaf of good sourdough with a golden crust.

butter
I always have good-quality butter in stock, for slathering on cobs of corn, or topping off baked potatoes. Unsalted butter is my preference, so I can control the amount of salt going into a dish.

dry rubs
You always want some good dry rubs on hand, whether you've made them yourself or bought them from a quality grocer. It's instant flavour for meats.

herbs
Whether it's chives, Italian parsley, dill or basil, fresh herbs should be available to finish a plate of grilled meats or veg, soup or a salad.

hot sauce

I love my hot sauces, and I keep a few of varying degrees of heat nearby. A couple of my essentials are Sriracha and sambal oelek.

kaffir lime leaves

These dark green leaves pack a ton of flavour and are an essential for Thai cooking. But you can use them in a variety of dishes, so keep them on hand for a citrus punch. They stay fresh in the freezer.

oils

I use good extra-virgin olive oil for salads and garnishing. For grilling, you want an oil with a high smoke point, such as canola or vegetable.

olives/cheese/charcuterie

Hungry guests have arrived at the door. Or maybe you'd rather do a picnic for dinner than a full-on meal. You'll find good olives, cheeses and cured meats are essential last-minute supplies for great meals.

salt

I'm a big believer in salting meats when they're finished, so I keep good fleur de sel, Maldon and kosher salts on hand. A good grind of pepper is always a nice finish, too.

sherry vinegar

This vinegar is a lot more versatile than the usual balsamic and can be used to season vegetables and meats and in salad dressings. It's my go-to vinegar.

stinky cheese

Limburger, Taleggio, Munster d'Alsace (not to be confused with regular Munster), Liederkranz—I love strong-smelling cheeses in their tangy, sharp, hoppy, rich-flavoured glory. Post-meal, I'd rather have cheese, fruit and good bread instead of dessert any day.

stock

I always keep homemade chicken and beef stocks (pp. 200 and 201) in the freezer, either in big batches or in ice cube trays, for when I just need a small amount.

brunch

green machine smoothie

8 kiwis, peeled
3 bananas
2 c packed spinach
1 c fresh or frozen chopped mangoes
1 c unsweetened almond milk
3 Tbsp coconut milk
¼ tsp spirulina powder

A couple of years ago, a lot of gyms were opening in our 'hood, so we added smoothies to our deli menu. We also give out smoothies upon arrival to students in our brunch class. To save time in the morning, purée all the ingredients in advance and pour into ice cube trays for freezing.

In a blender, combine ingredients and purée until desired consistency is reached.

540 beety smoothie

1 c orange juice
1 red beet, chopped (5 oz)
1 Tbsp grated ginger
1 lb fresh or frozen mangoes
5 oz fresh or frozen pineapple
4 mint leaves
⅔ c coconut water

This is a definite meal-on-the-go. You could even transform the purée into frozen treats. For Sunday brunch, take it up a notch with a little Pernod or sambuca—licorice notes are a natural with the sweet yet earthy beet flavour.

In a high-power blender, combine orange juice, beets and ginger and blend on high for 2 minutes, until smooth. Add remaining ingredients and blend for another 3 minutes.

CHEF'S NOTE
This smoothie can be poured into ice cube trays and frozen for up to 8 weeks. When ready to use, remove frozen smoothie from the trays and blend with more coconut water until the desired consistency is reached.

crème brûlée French toast

Our pastry chef Kat created this recipe for my daughter Chase. Every year, we prepare a cheap and cheerful Christmas breakfast at her school, and this dish is a major hit with the kids, but it's sophisticated enough for a grown-up's brunch. The longer the bread soaks, the more it will resemble crème brûlée rather than French toast. Make it in batches and keep them warm in the oven.

French toast In a large bowl, combine both sugars, vanilla paste, fleur de sel, half-and-half and eggs and mix well. Set aside.

Cut bread slices diagonally into two triangles. Overlap slices in a baking pan, like shingles, with points facing up. Pour egg mixture overtop, making sure bread is completely soaked. Press bread into the mixture if needed. Wrap in plastic wrap and refrigerate for at least 1 hour, but preferably overnight.

Remove pan from the refrigerator and set aside at room temperature for 30 minutes.

Preheat oven to 350°F.

Bake for 25 to 30 minutes, until centre is cooked through (when a knife inserted into the mixture comes out clean). Set aside and leave the oven on.

toffee sauce In a saucepan, combine all ingredients and bring to a boil. Reduce heat to medium-low and simmer for 2 minutes, until sugar is dissolved and sauce has thickened slightly.

assembly Immediately pour hot toffee sauce on top of the French toast. Return to the oven and bake until toffee sauce bubbles and clings to the surface. Serve hot with your favourite French toast toppings, such as whipped cream, fresh fruit or Hazelnut Praline.

French toast
2/3 c packed brown sugar
1/2 c granulated sugar
1 tsp vanilla paste
1 tsp fleur de sel
4 c half-and-half cream
12 large eggs
1 Pullman loaf, sliced and crusts removed

toffee sauce
3/4 c packed brown sugar
6 Tbsp unsalted butter
1 Tbsp heavy (36%) cream
3/4 tsp fleur de sel

assembly
whipped cream
fresh fruit
Hazelnut Praline
(p. 186, optional)

brunch

anything goes

Brunch has come a long way from the formal steam table loaded with eggs Benedict and stacks of buttermilk pancakes. Today's brunch is a full-on culinary celebration for people who are perfectly willing to stand in line for an hour to get a feast that's a little special, but without paying dinnertime prices. For some, it's also a chance to drink before noon. In other words, it's culinary daytime decadence, an opportunity to socialize and the most laid-back meal of the day, without rules and formalities, which might be why it's become the Millennial's weekly—or daily—ritual. And I can understand that, because when I was a kid, my favourite meal of all time was when my parents were low on groceries and breakfast was served for dinner. Breakfast foods are now all-day foods.

That means limitless menu options at brunch: from healthy, lighter fare such as a beet smoothie (p. 18) and Togarashi-Grilled Tuna Brioche with Pickled Veg and Ginger Aoli (p. 34) to hearty meals like Crispy Porchetta and Fried Egg with Shaved Fennel and Apples (p. 30) and Huevos Rancheros (p. 29). Cured salmon earns a place on every brunch menu simply because it's both healthy and versatile—it can be folded into an eggs Benny, scrambled with soft and buttery eggs or stacked high on a flaky biscuit (p. 25).

And then there's the decadent side of the brunch trend. As a culture, we're often contradicting ourselves because we're emphasizing "clean eating," while at the same time looking for original dining experiences. Personally, I roll both ways. Brunch is a great time to indulge in a hit of sweetness with Brown Sugar Bacon (p. 22) or dig into a rich, savoury meal of steak with aioli (p. 23). Some weekends, I'm all for a simple protein-packed smoothie to sustain me. Other days I might just want to go all out. One day at the Dirty Apron, a happy group of tourists brought in a bottle of wine at brunch and ordered everything off the menu. Why not? It's the one meal where you can eat guilt-free, because you've got the rest of the day to burn it off.

brown sugar bacon

serves 2

¼ cup brown sugar

4 slices thick-cut double-smoked bacon, about ½ inch thick

At our deli, customers will often order a few slabs of this to go. It's so delicious I'm guessing they eat it before they make it home. The caramelization and salty-sweet goodness of double-smoked bacon is simply the perfect bite.

Put brown sugar in a small saucepan, add ¼ cup water and heat over medium heat. Cook 45 seconds, until sugar has dissolved and large simmering bubbles form. Turn off heat and allow the mixture to cool.

In a separate frying pan over high heat, sear bacon for 1 minute. Flip over and cook for another minute, until the edges turn crispy. Cook for another 3 to 4 minutes, then pour in the sugar mixture and coat both sides. Turn off heat to prevent the mixture from burning. (Alternatively, the brown sugar mixture can be brushed onto the bacon and baked in a 400°F oven for 10 to 12 minutes. Bake until bacon has reached desired crispiness.) Cool down slightly, then serve.

Thai beef steak sandwich with lemongrass aioli

serves 4

When *The Dirty Apron Cookbook* was released, the roast chicken sandwich was our bestseller. These days, our Thai beef steak sandwich tops that list. It's super versatile and each component of this dish can be used in another dish. There are a few steps involved, but the results are so tasty it's worth the effort.

Thai beef Add all ingredients except the steak to a blender and purée on high speed for 3 to 4 minutes. Transfer to a bowl and add steak, coating both sides. Cover with plastic wrap and refrigerate for 24 hours.

Preheat grill over high heat to 400°F.

Remove steak from the marinade and pat dry. Transfer the remaining marinade to a small saucepan and bring to a boil. Immediately turn off the heat and set aside.

Place steak on the grill and grill each side for 4 minutes, 8 minutes in total, or until the internal temperature reaches 125°F on a meat thermometer. Transfer to a cutting board and set aside to cool to room temperature.

Cut steak into ¼-inch-thick slices. Transfer steak slices to a bowl, add 3 tablespoons of cooked marinade and evenly coat slices. Set aside.

lemongrass aioli In a blender, combine all ingredients except the mayonnaise, and blend on high until smooth. Fold in the mayonnaise and set aside.

Sriracha-honey-lime vinaigrette In a medium bowl, combine all ingredients and whisk until well mixed. Set aside. (Dressing can be stored in the refrigerator for up to 2 months.)

sandwich In a small bowl, combine papaya and onion. Mix with Sriracha-honey-lime dressing until evenly coated.

Slice each baguette portion in half lengthwise without cutting all the way through. Press open, then spread each side with lemongrass aioli and top with peanuts, steak, papaya, onion and Thai basil leaves.

Thai beef
½ c fish sauce
½ c oyster sauce
½ c granulated palm sugar
¼ c coarsely chopped garlic
¼ c thinly sliced lemongrass
1 tsp ground white pepper
1 lb hanger steak

lemongrass aioli
¼ c chopped cilantro
2 Tbsp chopped lemongrass
1 Tbsp kaffir lime leaves
1 Tbsp grated ginger
1 Tbsp fresh lime juice
½ c mayonnaise

Sriracha-honey-lime vinaigrette
1½ Tbsp honey
1½ Tbsp fresh lime juice
2 tsp soy sauce
2 tsp Sriracha
2 tsp rice vinegar
1 tsp sesame oil

sandwich
¼ green papaya, cut into thin strips
1 red onion, thinly sliced
1 Tbsp Sriracha-Honey-Lime Vinaigrette (see here)
2 (12-inch) baguettes, halved widthwise
½ c Lemongrass Aioli (see here)
¼ c toasted peanuts
Thai Beef (see here)
24 Thai basil leaves

gravlax and breakfast biscuits

This recipe is about the butter in the biscuit, which makes it light and flaky and pairs so well with the saltiness of the salmon. But take note: gravlax needs two days' prep, so this is not a last-minute dish.

gravlax Pat salmon fillet with paper towel to remove moisture.

In a frying pan, combine coriander seeds, fennel seeds and star anise and toast over medium-high heat for 1 minute. (Careful not to burn.) Set aside to cool, then use a mortar and pestle to coarsely crush the spices.

In a small bowl, combine spices, salt, sugar, dill and lemon and lime zests and mix thoroughly.

Line a roasting pan with a large piece of plastic wrap (enough to overlap the salmon). Place a quarter of the curing mixture on the bottom and spread out loosely. Place fillet, skin-side down, onto the curing mixture, then pour remaining mixture over fillet and evenly spread out until salmon is completely covered. Wrap plastic wrap tightly around the fish. Place another roasting pan on top and add 5 pounds of weights to it, to press the salmon while curing. Refrigerate for 48 hours.

Lightly rinse curing mixture off the salmon under cold running water. Pat dry and thinly slice on an angle. Set aside. (This makes enough for 8 to 10 servings, but leftover cured salmon can be covered with plastic wrap and refrigerated for 3 weeks or frozen for 6 weeks. If frozen, defrost it overnight and slice the next day.)

biscuits In a mixing bowl, sift together flour, salt, baking powder and baking soda.

In a food processor with an S-shaped blade attachment, pulse the flour mixture and butter in batches until the butter cubes are a quarter their original size. Transfer mixture to a large bowl.

Pour in buttermilk and mix well, until dough looks shaggy and barely holds together. (Add more buttermilk if needed.) Do not knead the dough—the larger the butter piece, the flakier the biscuits will be.

continued overleaf

gravlax

1 (3-lb) sockeye salmon fillet, skin on and pin bones removed

1 Tbsp coriander seeds

1 Tbsp fennel seeds

6 star anise

1 c kosher salt

1¼ c brown sugar

bunch of dill, coarsely chopped

grated zest of 1 lime

grated zest of 1 lemon

biscuits

5⅔ c all-purpose flour, plus extra for dusting

1¾ tsp kosher salt, plus extra for the egg wash

4 tsp baking powder

1½ tsp baking soda

2½ c (5 sticks) unsalted butter, cut into ½-inch cubes and frozen

2 c buttermilk, plus extra if needed (divided)

2 egg yolks

continued overleaf

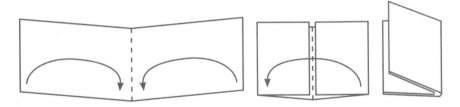

lemon mascarpone

2 c mascarpone cheese

1 Tbsp maple syrup

1 tsp kosher salt

grated zest of 1 lemon

assembly

¼ c Lemon Mascarpone
(see here)

4 Biscuits (see here), halved

1 vine-ripened tomato,
quartered and sliced

1 avocado, sliced

12 slices Gravlax (see here)

4 eggs, cooked sunny-side up

kosher salt and ground
black pepper, to taste

1 Tbsp chopped chives

Place dough on a lightly floured work surface and pat it into a rectangular shape. Roll dough to a ¼-inch thickness. Fold ends to the centre, then fold in half like a book. Cover and refrigerate for at least 30 minutes. Repeat procedure three times. (The pastry must rest to relax gluten and prevent dough from shrinking too much.)

Preheat oven to 400°F. Line a baking sheet with parchment paper.

Roll the dough out to 6 × 18 inches. Using a sharp knife, cut the dough into twelve 3-inch squares. (Avoid any sawing or circular motions, as they may destroy the layers you've been working hard to create.)

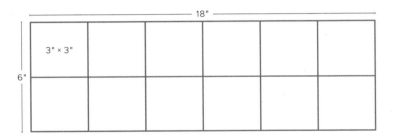

In a small bowl, combine egg yolks, a pinch of salt, and 2 tablespoons water. Mix, then strain to remove the chalaza. Put biscuits on the prepared baking sheet and brush with egg wash. Put the biscuits in the oven, reduce the temperature to 375°F and bake for 15 to 20 minutes until golden brown and internal temperature reaches 195°F.

lemon mascarpone Combine ingredients in a medium bowl and mix well. Set aside. (Makes 2 cups.)

assembly Spread lemon mascarpone on the cut sides of each biscuit. Add a few slices of tomato and avocado to the bottom half of each biscuit. Layer three slices of gravlax and a sunny-side up egg on top. Season with salt and pepper and garnish with chives. Top with the other biscuit half and enjoy warm!

huevos rancheros

This Mexican breakfast dish is a diner staple, probably because it's so simple and delicious, with rich egg yolk and buttery avocado. If you're hosting a brunch, you can prepare the sauce a couple of days ahead.

jalapeño–ancho chili sauce In a medium bowl, combine all ingredients except the chili powder, lime juice, salt and pepper. Using an immersion blender or stand blender, purée mixture until smooth. Add chili powder and lime juice, season with salt and pepper and mix well. Set aside or refrigerate until needed.

huevos rancheros Fill a large saucepan with 3 inches of water, add vinegar and bring to a boil. Reduce heat to a gentle simmer.

Meanwhile, in a large skillet over medium-high heat, combine cumin seeds and cinnamon stick and toast for 2 minutes, or until fragrant. Reduce heat to low, add oil, onions, garlic and bay leaves and sauté for 3 to 4 minutes, until onions are translucent. (Careful not to burn.)

Add red peppers and jalapeños to the pan and sauté for another minute. (If pan is dry, add a little more oil.) Add tomatoes and simmer for 5 to 10 minutes. Stir in chorizo and crushed red pepper flakes and simmer for another 2 to 3 minutes, until it has a salsa-like consistency. (If the tomato sauce becomes dry, add water to loosen it up.)

Remove bay leaves and cinnamon stick and season to taste with salt, pepper and lime juice.

Crack an egg into a small bowl and gently slide it into the simmering water. Cook for 15 to 20 seconds, until the whites begin to solidify. Add the next egg. And repeat with the remainder. Poach for 3 to 4 minutes, until the whites are completely opaque but the yolks are still soft. Using a slotted spoon, remove eggs from the water and gently pat dry with a paper towel.

assembly Ladle tomato-pepper sauce into 4 shallow bowls. Place 2 poached eggs on top of each serving, then spoon on jalapeño–ancho chili sauce and top with sliced avocado and cilantro. Serve with tortillas, crispy ciabatta or sourdough.

jalapeño–ancho chili sauce

- ½ c extra-virgin olive oil
- ½ c Italian parsley leaves
- 2 anchovy fillets
- 2 cloves garlic, finely chopped
- ½ jalapeño, finely chopped
- 3 Tbsp capers
- 4 tsp grainy mustard
- 2 tsp ancho chili powder
- juice of ½ lime
- kosher salt and coarsely ground black pepper, to taste

huevos rancheros

- 2 Tbsp white wine vinegar
- 4 tsp cumin seeds
- ½ cinnamon stick
- 2 Tbsp olive oil, plus extra if needed
- 1 small onion, chopped
- 4 cloves garlic, finely chopped
- 2 bay leaves
- 1 red bell pepper, seeded, deveined and cut into a ½-inch dice
- 3 Tbsp finely chopped jalapeños
- 2 c canned tomatoes with their juices, crushed
- ⅔ c finely chopped Spanish chorizo
- pinch of crushed red pepper flakes
- kosher salt and ground black pepper, to taste
- juice of 1 lime
- 8 eggs
- 1 avocado, sliced, for garnish
- cilantro, for garnish
- tortillas, crispy ciabatta or sourdough, to serve

crispy porchetta and fried egg with shaved fennel and apples

pictured p. 33
serves 10 to 12

This dish illustrates how a dinner can transform into brunch with the simple addition of an egg. The apple cider vinaigrette and the greens balance out the fattiness of the crispy, savoury pork.
You can request your cut of pork belly from your butcher two to three days in advance to guarantee the cut.

chimichurri

1 shallot, roughly chopped

2 cloves garlic, roughly chopped

2 Tbsp fresh oregano leaves

pinch of crushed red pepper flakes

½ c extra-virgin olive oil

3 Tbsp sherry vinegar, plus extra to taste

1 c Italian parsley leaves

kosher salt, to taste

crispy porchetta

5½ lbs pork belly

3 Tbsp Chimichurri (see here)

6 cloves garlic, finely chopped

grated zest of 1 lemon

8 sprigs thyme, leaves only

2 sprigs rosemary, leaves only

2 Tbsp fleur de sel (divided)

1 tsp fennel seeds

1 tsp ground black pepper

pinch of crushed red pepper flakes

2 Tbsp vegetable oil

arugula salad

3 Tbsp apple cider vinegar

3 Tbsp extra-virgin olive oil

kosher salt and ground black pepper, to taste

4 c arugula

1 large Granny Smith apple, unpeeled and shaved on a mandoline

1 large bulb fennel, shaved on a mandoline

continued facing

chimichurri In a food processor, combine all ingredients except for the parsley and salt. Pulse for 30 seconds. Add parsley and pulse for another 30 seconds, until smooth. (Careful not to over-purée, or your chimichurri will turn black.) Season with salt and add more sherry vinegar, if needed.

crispy porchetta Dry the pork belly with paper towel. Using a very sharp knife, score the surface of the pork skin, with evenly spaced cuts ½ inch apart.

Rub chimichurri on the flesh side, leaving a ½-inch space around the edges. In a small bowl, combine garlic, lemon zest, thyme, rosemary, 1 tablespoon fleur de sel, fennel seeds, pepper and crushed red pepper flakes. Sprinkle mixture on top.

Roll pork belly lengthwise, like a Swiss roll (see photos). Be sure to wrap butcher twine around the pork loin several times, along the loin, and knot the end. (This keeps the loin together and prevents it from opening while cooking.)

Transfer pork belly to a baking sheet and air-dry, uncovered, in the refrigerator for 24 hours. Remove pork belly from the refrigerator and set aside at room temperature for 1 hour.

Preheat oven to 475°F.

Drizzle the outside of the pork belly with oil and sprinkle with remaining tablespoon of fleur de sel. Roast uncovered in the oven for 15 minutes, rotate

CHEF'S NOTE
This recipe requires a spool of butcher's twine.

baking sheet 180 degrees and roast for another 15 minutes. (This will ensure even roasting.) Rotate baking sheet again, reduce temperature to 325°F and roast for another hour, or until the internal temperature reaches 145°F on a meat thermometer. Set aside to rest for 20 minutes.

arugula salad Whisk vinegar, oil, salt and pepper together and set aside. Combine arugula, apple and fennel in a bowl. Dress with the vinaigrette.

assembly Slice porchetta into ¼-inch rounds. Place a slice on each plate and top with a handful of the salad and an egg. Finish with salt and pepper.

assembly
10 to 12 large eggs, sunny-side up
kosher salt and ground black pepper, to taste

**crispy porchetta
and fried egg
with shaved fennel
and apples**

p. 30

brunch

togarashi-grilled tuna brioche
with pickled veg and ginger aioli

serves 4

pickled vegetables

⅓ c red wine vinegar

⅓ c granulated sugar

2 carrots, cut into thin strips

1 daikon, cut into thin strips

2 (8-fl oz) sterilized canning jars with sealable lids

pickled ginger aioli

¼ c strained pickled ginger

1 c mayonnaise

½ tsp ginger powder

togarashi-grilled albacore tuna

12 oz albacore tuna loins

¼ c togarashi

4 tsp sea salt

4 tsp vegetable oil

½ c Pickled Ginger Aioli (see here)

4 Tomato Sesame Brioche Buns (p. 164), halved

½ c Pickled Vegetables (see here)

2 avocados, sliced

2 c arugula, loosely packed

1 c nori seaweed, cut into thin strips

We invented this dish—as the perfect beach-style sandwich— at our pop-up tent for the Harmony Arts Festival in West Vancouver. The bun is a toasty bed for the rich aioli, the crunch of the pickles and the seasoned tuna. *Togarashi*, a Japanese seasoning blend of chiles, orange peel and nori, can be found in larger supermarkets and Asian grocery stores.

pickled vegetables Combine vinegar and sugar in a small saucepan over medium heat and stir until sugar is dissolved. (Do not allow to boil.) Remove from heat and set aside to cool completely.

Place carrots and daikon in sterilized canning jars and cover with the sweetened vinegar. Seal tightly and refrigerate for at least 24 hours. (They can be refrigerated for up to 3 months.)

pickled ginger aioli Combine all ingredients in a blender and purée on medium-high until smooth and spreadable. (Makes 1 cup.)

togarashi-grilled albacore tuna Preheat grill over high heat to 400°F.

Season tuna loins with togarashi and salt, then brush with oil on both sides. Sear each side of the tuna loin for 30 seconds, ensuring that it's still quite rare. Set aside to cool. Slice into ¼-inch-thick slices.

Spread aioli on both faces of the brioche buns, add tuna, pickled vegetables, avocado and arugula, then top with nori. Close up the sandwiches and serve!

Spanish-style grilled octopus and lemon aioli

p. 38

brunch

Spanish-style grilled octopus and lemon aioli

pictured p. 37
serves 4

smoked paprika vinaigrette
2 cloves garlic, finely chopped
grated zest and juice of 1 lemon
2 Tbsp extra-virgin olive oil
2 tsp sherry vinegar
1 tsp smoked sweet paprika
kosher salt and ground black pepper, to taste

lemon aioli
½ c mayonnaise
grated zest and juice of 1 lemon
1 clove garlic, finely chopped
kosher salt and ground black pepper, to taste

deep-fried garlic chips
8 cloves garlic
½ c milk
2 c canola oil

deep-fried capers and parsley
reserved cooking oil from garlic chips
¼ c capers
¼ c Italian parsley leaves

continued facing

People love octopus. It touches my chef heart when even my young daughter Dylan orders it in a restaurant. Don't be intimidated. It's all about cooking it whole, tenderizing it low and slow in the oven and getting a bit of char off the barbecue, which is where the flavours develop. Be sure to clean the tentacles thoroughly before cooking.

smoked paprika vinaigrette Combine all ingredients in a bowl and whisk together.

lemon aioli Combine all ingredients in a bowl and mix together. Adjust seasoning to taste.

deep-fried garlic chips With a mandoline or sharp knife, carefully slice garlic as thin as possible. In a small bowl, combine garlic and milk and soak for 12 to 24 hours.

In a small saucepan, heat oil to a temperature of 325°F. (Use a thermometer for an accurate reading.) Drain garlic, then spread onto a paper towel and pat dry. Using a slotted spoon, carefully lower garlic into oil and deep-fry for 1½ to 2 minutes, until golden brown. Transfer chips onto a paper towel–lined plate and set aside to cool. Reserve cooking oil.

deep-fried capers and parsley In a small saucepan, heat oil to a temperature of 325°F. (Use a thermometer for an accurate reading.) Using a slotted spoon, carefully lower capers into the oil and deep-fry for 10 seconds. Transfer to a paper towel–lined plate.

Add parsley leaves to the oil and deep-fry for 45 seconds, until they stop bubbling. Using a slotted spoon, transfer leaves to the same plate.

octopus Preheat oven to 250°F.

Season octopus with lemon juice, salt and pepper. Wrap in aluminum foil, making sure to seal the foil around the octopus completely. Place it on a baking sheet and bake on the lower rack of the oven, near the back, for 2½ to 3 hours, or until tender.

Remove from the oven and set aside to cool to room temperature. Cut octopus into 2-inch strips.

assembly Preheat grill over high heat to 400°F.

Place potatoes in a saucepan of cold salted water and bring to a boil. Reduce heat to medium-low and simmer for 20 to 25 minutes, until cooked through. (To test doneness, pierce with a fork and the potato should slide off with little resistance.) Drain, then cool potatoes on a baking sheet. Slice in half lengthwise.

In a small bowl, combine octopus and potatoes and season with salt, pepper and olive oil.

Place octopus and potatoes onto a hot spot on the grill and char for 1 minute, until slightly crispy. Flip over and char for another minute. Transfer octopus and potatoes to a bowl, add smoked paprika vinaigrette and gently toss. Add chopped parsley and season to taste.

Garnish with deep-fried capers, parsley and garlic chips. Serve with lemon aioli.

octopus

2 lb raw octopus, tentacles and body only

juice of 2 lemons

kosher salt and ground black pepper, to taste

assembly

8 fingerling potatoes

1 lb cooked Octopus (see here)

kosher salt and ground black pepper, to taste

1½ Tbsp extra-virgin olive oil

3 Tbsp Smoked Paprika Vinaigrette (see here)

2 Tbsp chopped Italian parsley

salads

broccolini and snap pea salad with tahini-soy dressing

serves 4

Broccolini is a relatively new vegetable hybrid—a little sweeter and more tender than broccoli, with a subtle asparagus taste. This is a perfect year-round salad: it's light and refreshing, but can hold up to roasted meats, grilled prawns or pan-seared fish.

tahini-soy dressing In a large bowl, combine all ingredients and whisk together until creamy in consistency.

salad Cut broccolini into thirds. Fill a large bowl with ice water. Bring a large saucepan of salted water to a boil and add broccolini and snap peas. Blanch for 15 seconds, then immediately transfer to the ice water bath.

Using a salad spinner, spin blanched snap peas and broccolini for 15 seconds, or until excess water is removed.

Add broccolini, snap peas and a pinch of salt to the tahini-soy dressing bowl and mix until evenly coated. Transfer to a serving dish and garnish with carrots, radish, toasted sesame seeds and parsley.

tahini-soy dressing
¼ cup tahini
¼ cup rice vinegar
2 Tbsp soy sauce
2 Tbsp maple syrup
1 Tbsp sesame oil
1 tsp togarashi

salad
2 bunches broccolini
1½ c snap peas, string removed
pinch of kosher salt
1 carrot, shaved
1 radish, thinly sliced
1 Tbsp toasted black and white sesame seeds
1 c Italian parsley leaves

Brussels sprouts salad

1½ litres vegetable oil
6 c Brussels sprouts
1 c Thai basil leaves (divided)
kosher salt, to taste
1 c chopped cilantro
2 Tbsp sesame seeds (divided)
¼ c Sriracha-Honey-Lime
Vinaigrette (p. 23)

This is my favourite salad—which is hard to believe, because as a kid I hated Brussels sprouts (they were often overcooked). They're hugely trendy right now, probably because they are so versatile. These ones are crispy fried goodness.

Heat oil in a deep-fryer or a deep saucepan over low heat to 300°F. (Use a thermometer for an accurate reading.) Line two baking sheets with paper towels.

Meanwhile, prep the Brussels sprouts. Trim off the tip end of each Brussels sprout and discard the outer layer of leaves. Peel off the second and third layers and reserve them in a small bowl. Cut the Brussels sprouts in half.

Carefully lower ½ cup of Thai basil into the oil and cook for 10 seconds, until leaves crisp. Using a slotted spoon, transfer Thai basil onto a prepared baking sheet. Sprinkle with salt.

Increase the temperature of the frying oil to 375°F. Carefully lower half of the halved Brussels sprouts into the oil and deep-fry for 3 minutes. Using a slotted spoon, transfer Brussels sprouts onto the other prepared baking sheet. Sprinkle with salt. Repeat with the remaining batch of halved Brussels sprouts.

In a large bowl, combine fried Brussels sprouts, reserved layers of Brussels sprout leaves, ½ cup Thai basil, cilantro, 1 tablespoon sesame seeds and vinaigrette. Mix until well combined and transfer into a serving dish. Garnish with remaining 1 tablespoon sesame seeds and fried Thai basil.

what is a salad?

They say that salads go as far back as the Romans, and English scholar John Evelyn likely wrote the first book on the subject in 1699. His book *Acetaria: A Discourse in Sallets* covers his passions for gardening and cooking, and his love of fresh, local ingredients. As an early advocate of the meatless diet, Evelyn possessed a large (and allegedly delicious) collection of vegetarian recipes. He might have been considered an eccentric by seventeenth-century standards, but he lived to the ripe old age of eighty-six, when the typical Englishman at the time was lucky if he made it to forty. That tells us a thing or two about a plant-based diet.

But what is a salad? *Merriam-Webster's* definitions of salad include raw greens combined with other raw veggies, tossed in dressing, or "small pieces of food" of any kind, mixed with dressing—or set in gelatin. But those definitions still don't really capture the broad umbrella term that is salad. Salad is so much more than greens tossed in a bowl with vinaigrette. The third definition is probably the best: "hodgepodge."

A salad can consist of veggies, fruits, meats, seafood, pasta, grains, nuts, seeds, dairy, egg, legumes and tofu. They can be raw, cooked, fermented or pickled, and chopped up in large pieces or finely grated. A potato salad has nothing in common with a chopped salad, other than the fact that they are both a hodgepodge of ingredients. But a salad can be a simple two- or three-ingredient dish, too—a quartered head of romaine can be grilled and drizzled in sauce and labelled a salad.

In fact, the only common denominator for this food grouping that I can think of is a mixture of ingredients with a light dressing that is evenly distributed, designed to marry the flavours together. Salads are all about diversity of textures and flavours, and, of course, seasonality. Base your choice of salad on whatever stands out at the local produce stand. If big, plump, juicy heirloom tomatoes and peaches are calling your name, then it's time to make Grilled Peach and Heirloom Tomato Salad (p. 55). And when the temperature drops, a roasted cauliflower salad with pickled sunflower seeds and pomegranate vinaigrette will brighten the day (p. 57).

But remember, a salad is also all about balance, about the textures and flavours melding together. One of my favourite combinations is something spicy, with something roasted or something toasted. The dressings are what pull the ingredients together, whether it's the zing of spicy harissa elevating some slightly caramelized, lemon-roasted baby carrots (p. 59) or the traditional Mexican pairing of cumin and lime with ripe, creamy avocado and the freshest, crispest greens (p. 50).

Ultimately, for me, a salad is feel-good food, and it shouldn't bog you down and leave you feeling full. It's an energizing food. And for the cook, salads offer a huge playground of options.

roasted Japanese eggplant and sesame salad with ginger dressing

serves 4

When it comes to a chef's favourite food item, eggplant is up there with kale. It's a versatile veg, and when quickly deep-fried (or roasted), the subtle flesh caramelizes. The sesame dressing brings nuttiness to the party.

ginger dressing In a small bowl, combine all ingredients and mix well. (The dressing can be refrigerated for up to 3 weeks.)

roasted Japanese eggplant and sesame salad Heat oil in a deep-fryer or deep saucepan to a temperature of 355°F. (Use a thermometer for an accurate reading.) Line a baking sheet with paper towels.

Meanwhile, cut the eggplants into thirds widthwise. Cut each section into long quarters.

Carefully lower eggplant into the oil and cook for 45 seconds to 1 minute, or until golden brown. Using tongs, carefully transfer eggplant to the prepared baking sheet.

In a large bowl, combine eggplant, endive, tomatoes, onions and Thai basil. Toss with the dressing. Transfer to a serving plate and sprinkle sesame seeds on top.

ginger dressing
¼ cup soy sauce
⅓ cup rice vinegar
1 Tbsp sesame oil
2 Tbsp grated ginger
2 Tbsp honey or maple syrup
2 cloves garlic, grated

roasted Japanese eggplant and sesame salad
4 c canola oil, for deep-frying
2 Japanese eggplants
1 purple or yellow Belgian endive, leaves separated
12 yellow cherry tomatoes, halved
12 red cherry tomatoes, halved
¼ red onion, thinly sliced
2 sprigs Thai basil, leaves only
1 Tbsp black and white sesame seeds, for sprinkling

CHEF'S NOTE
For a healthier option, the eggplants can be roasted in a preheated oven at 425°F for 7 to 8 minutes.

local greens, avocado and feta salad with cumin-lime vinaigrette

serves 4

cumin-lime vinaigrette

½ cup extra-virgin olive oil

juice of 2 limes

1 tsp ground cumin, plus extra to taste

1 tsp cumin seeds

pinch of crushed red pepper flakes, plus extra to taste

kosher salt and ground black pepper, to taste

salad

2 heads mixed live lettuce

1 avocado, sliced

2 c cherry tomatoes, halved

½ c cilantro leaves

½ shallot, thinly sliced

½ c feta cheese, crumbled

This fresh, flavourful salad speaks of the season's best. Here, we use live lettuce heads to up the fresh factor, but with the great urban farmers' markets these days, you can grab everything from microgreens to pea shoots to dandelions and they'll taste great. Cumin works well in vinaigrettes, so don't be afraid to use it.

cumin-lime vinaigrette In a small bowl, combine all ingredients and whisk until well mixed. Season to taste with more cumin, red pepper flakes, salt and/or pepper.

salad Soak heads of lettuce in cold water for 30 minutes to make the leaves crispier. Remove roots and roughly chop. Swish lettuce around in cold water for another 3 minutes to remove any excess dirt. Drain, then transfer lettuce to a salad spinner and spin for 30 seconds to remove any excess water.

In a large bowl, combine lettuce, avocado, tomatoes, cilantro, shallot and feta. Add the cumin-lime vinaigrette and toss until thoroughly mixed. Transfer to a serving bowl.

edamame and soba noodle salad
with ginger-sesame vinaigrette

Topped with tofu, chicken, beef or fish, this salad is a meal unto itself. It also travels well, so bring it to the beach or a picnic. If you want a gluten-free version, be sure to look for 100 per cent buckwheat noodles. Contrary to its name, buckwheat is not a grain, so it's fine for anyone with gluten sensitivities. It's also a superfood and rich in nutrients.

ginger-sesame vinaigrette In a medium bowl, combine all ingredients and whisk until well mixed. Set aside.

edamame and soba noodle salad Bring a saucepan of water to a boil. Add soba noodles and cook for 4 to 5 minutes, until cooked through. Drain in a colander, then rinse under cold running water.

In a large bowl, combine noodles, carrots, green onions, snap peas, edamame, sesame seeds and dressing and toss well. Season with salt and pepper. Transfer to a serving dish and serve.

ginger-sesame vinaigrette

¼ cup soy sauce

⅓ cup rice vinegar

2 Tbsp mirin

2 Tbsp grated ginger

2 tsp sesame oil

edamame and soba noodle salad

4 oz soba noodles

1 small carrot, cut into thin strips

2 green onions, cut into thin strips

1 c snap peas, string removed and cut into thin strips

½ c shelled edamame

1 Tbsp black and white sesame seeds

kosher salt and ground black pepper, to taste

kabocha and wild rice salad

spiced pumpkin seeds
¼ cup shelled pumpkin seeds
½ Tbsp curry powder
½ tsp chili powder
1 Tbsp maple syrup
1 tsp sherry vinegar
pinch of salt

roasted kabocha squash
Small kabocha squash, unpeeled, seeded and cut into 1-inch pieces
2 Tbsp maple syrup
2 Tbsp sherry vinegar
kosher salt and ground black pepper, to taste
2 Tbsp extra-virgin olive oil

wild rice
1 c wild rice
1 tsp kosher salt

cranberry-champagne vinaigrette
¼ cup dried cranberries
⅔ cup olive oil
⅓ cup champagne vinegar
kosher salt and ground black pepper, to taste

assembly
Italian parsley leaves, for garnish
shaved Parmesan cheese, for garnish

The beauty of this dish is you can easily switch out the kabocha squash for butternut or acorn. This is a substantial salad, particularly great from late fall to winter when the weather starts to cool and we want something hearty. And the spiced pumpkin seeds are also a tasty snack on their own.

spiced pumpkin seeds Preheat oven to 350°F. Line a baking sheet with parchment paper.

In a small bowl, combine all ingredients and mix well. Set aside for 30 minutes, or until pumpkin seeds soak up the liquid. Transfer mixture to the prepared baking sheet and spread out. Bake for 10 minutes. Remove from oven and set aside.

roasted kabocha squash Preheat oven to 425°F.

In a medium bowl, combine all ingredients and toss until the squash is coated. Transfer squash mixture to a baking sheet and roast for 20 to 25 minutes until squash is cooked through and slightly caramelized.

wild rice Place wild rice in a sieve and rinse well under cold running water.

In a deep saucepan, combine rice, salt and 2 litres cold water and bring to a boil. Reduce heat to medium-low and simmer, covered, for 1 hour, until cooked through. Drain wild rice and set aside.

cranberry-champagne vinaigrette In a small bowl, combine all ingredients and whisk until well mixed.

assembly In a bowl, combine wild rice and vinaigrette and mix well. Add roasted squash and spiced pumpkin seeds. Transfer to a serving plate and garnish with parsley and shaved Parmesan.

grilled peach and heirloom tomato salad

serves 3 to 4

If you've never grilled fruit, this is the time to try it. When the beautiful natural sugars in the peach are charred, it develops another dimension of flavour. Play around with this one using any other high-sugar fruit, such as pineapple, pears or apricots.

Preheat grill over high heat to 400°F.

In a small bowl, combine peaches, oil, salt and pepper and toss until wedges are evenly coated. Place peaches, flesh-side down, on the grill and grill for 25 seconds. Flip and grill for another 25 seconds. Transfer peaches to a medium bowl.

Add tomatoes, basil, lemon juice and spiced pumpkin seeds and toss. Season with salt and pepper to taste.

Transfer salad to a serving plate and garnish with watercress and goat cheese.

2 large ripe peaches, pitted and each cut into eight wedges

3 Tbsp extra-virgin olive oil

kosher salt and ground black pepper, to taste

2 large heirloom tomatoes, cut into bite-size pieces

12 basil leaves

2 Tbsp fresh lemon juice

¼ c Spiced Pumpkin Seeds (p. 52)

½ c loosely packed watercress

¼ c goat cheese, crumbled

okra chickpea salad

okra chickpea salad

24 okra

6 Tbsp extra-virgin olive oil (divided)

kosher salt and ground black pepper, to taste

2 c canola oil, for deep-frying

¼ c cooked Chickpeas (p. 198)

12 yellow cherry tomatoes, halved

12 red cherry tomatoes, halved

½ c thinly sliced red onion

1 tsp grated garlic

1 tsp grated ginger

1 tsp Espelette pepper

3 Tbsp sherry vinegar

¼ c cilantro leaves

This is one of my "refrigerator salads," which means I came up with it after searching through my refrigerator one night to see what I had in stock. This unorthodox recipe has ingredients from around the world, but it works—and the vinaigrette makes it a refreshingly light meal. Plus, grilling the okra takes away the slightly slimy texture of the raw vegetable.

okra chickpea salad Preheat grill over high heat to 400°F.

Trim off stems of okra. In a medium bowl, combine okra, 3 tablespoons olive oil, salt and pepper and toss well. Place okra on the grill and grill for 2 minutes per side. Transfer okra to a clean bowl to cool.

Heat oil in a deep fryer or deep saucepan to 375°F. (Use a thermometer for an accurate reading.) Carefully lower chickpeas into the oil and deep-fry for 3 minutes. Using a slotted spoon, transfer chickpeas to a plate lined with paper towels.

In a large bowl, combine okra, tomatoes, onions, garlic, ginger, Espelette pepper, the remaining 3 tablespoons olive oil and vinegar and toss well. Season with salt, then transfer to a serving plate and garnish with crispy chickpeas and cilantro.

roasted cauliflower with pickled sunflower seeds and pomegranate vinaigrette

serves 4

Cauliflower is one of those veggies that takes on a nutty, caramelized taste when roasted, and the acidity of the pickled seeds and fresh pomegranate adds layers of flavour.

pickled sunflower seeds In a small bowl, combine all ingredients and mix well. Set aside for 30 minutes at room temperature, then drain and set sunflower seeds aside.

pomegranate vinaigrette In a small bowl, combine all ingredients and whisk until well mixed.

roasted cauliflower Preheat oven to 425°F.

In a large bowl, combine cauliflower, oil, sumac, salt and pepper and toss well. Transfer to a baking sheet and roast for 15 to 17 minutes, until lightly browned. Set aside to cool to room temperature.

assembly Put cauliflower back into the large bowl and add just enough pomegranate vinaigrette to coat. Add pickled sunflower seeds and pomegranate seeds. Add mint and cilantro and toss, then transfer to a serving dish.

pickled sunflower seeds
2 Tbsp sunflower seeds
2 Tbsp fresh lemon juice
½ tsp extra-virgin olive oil
pinch of salt

pomegranate vinaigrette
3 Tbsp olive oil
1 Tbsp pomegranate molasses
1 Tbsp maple syrup
1 tsp sumac
1 tsp harissa paste or powder
pinch of salt
juice of ½ lemon

roasted cauliflower
1 cauliflower (about 3 lbs), cleaned and broken into florets
1 Tbsp extra-virgin olive oil
1 tsp sumac
kosher salt and ground black pepper, to taste

assembly
½ c pomegranate seeds
¼ c mint leaves
¼ c cilantro leaves

lemon-roasted baby carrots with harissa vinaigrette

serves 4 to 6

This isn't the tired orange-juice-honey-roasted carrot recipe your mom taught you. Harissa is a thick chili pepper paste made with garlic and aromatic spices, and these carrots are elevated with the exotic flavours of the Middle East. We use multicolored carrots for colour, but if they're unavailable orange baby carrots will also do nicely.

lemon-roasted baby carrots Preheat oven to 450°F. In a bowl, combine all ingredients and toss until evenly coated. Roast on a baking sheet for 15 to 20 minutes, until tender. Set aside to cool.

harissa vinaigrette In a medium bowl, combine oil, vinegars, lemon juice and harissa and mix well. Season with salt and pepper, then set aside.

lemon yogurt In a small bowl, mix yogurt with lemon zest and juice. Set aside.

assembly In a bowl, combine carrots, chickpeas, spices, herbs and vinaigrette and toss. Transfer to a serving plate and garnish with herbs and lemon yogurt.

lemon-roasted baby carrots
20 multicoloured baby carrots

2 Tbsp sherry vinegar

2 Tbsp honey

2 Tbsp fresh lemon juice

2 Tbsp olive oil

kosher salt and ground black pepper, to taste

harissa vinaigrette
½ c olive oil

2 Tbsp rice vinegar

2 Tbsp sherry vinegar

2 Tbsp fresh lemon juice

2 tsp harissa

kosher salt and ground black pepper, to taste

lemon yogurt
½ c plain yogurt

grated zest and juice of 1 lemon

assembly
2 Tbsp cooked Chickpeas (p. 198)

1 tsp toasted fennel seeds, coarsely ground

1 tsp toasted coriander seeds, coarsely ground

1 tsp sumac

1 Tbsp chopped Italian parsley, plus extra for garnish

1 Tbsp chopped cilantro, plus extra for garnish

1 Tbsp chopped mint, plus extra for garnish

soups

serves 6 **avgolemono**

2 Tbsp olive oil

1 large onion, chopped

1 carrot, chopped

3 stalks celery, chopped

3 bay leaves

6 cloves garlic, finely chopped

½ c white wine

2 litres Chicken Stock (p. 200)

grated zest and juice of
2 lemons

1 Tbsp oregano

2 c roasted chicken thigh meat,
cut into bite-size pieces

2 c kale, stems removed and
coarsely chopped

½ c cooked basmati rice

kosher salt and ground black
pepper, to taste

We've come up with our version of this Greek feel-good soup, with the perfect tartness and acidity. It's a light and refreshing soup because we omit the traditional egg yolk. And with the chicken and rice, it's also a one-pot meal.

Heat oil in a large saucepan over medium heat. Add onions, carrots, celery and bay leaves and sauté for 3 to 4 minutes. Add garlic and sauté for 30 seconds.

Pour in wine and cook for another 2 minutes, until liquid has reduced by half. Pour in stock and simmer for 8 to 10 minutes, until vegetables are cooked.

Stir in lemon zest and juice, oregano and chicken. Turn heat off. Add kale and rice and season with salt and pepper. Stir well, then ladle soup into bowls. Enjoy!

serves 6 to 8   toasted cumin and eggplant soup

With the mint and cumin flavours, this soup also doubles as a great sauce for grilled meats. It has a subtle smokiness that comes through, and it's a great example of how toasting seeds can enhance a dish.

mint oil Fill a bowl with ice water and set aside.

Bring a saucepan of water to a boil. Add mint leaves and boil for 30 seconds. Using a slotted spoon, transfer mint to the ice bath and allow to sit for 30 seconds. Transfer mint to a blender, add oil and purée until smooth.

Strain mixture into a small bowl and set aside until needed.

toasted cumin and eggplant soup Preheat oven to 425°F. Line a baking sheet with parchment paper.

In a large bowl, combine eggplant, 2 tablespoons oil, cumin, red pepper flakes and salt and toss well to evenly coat the eggplant. Transfer eggplant to the prepared baking sheet and roast for 20 minutes.

Once eggplants have been roasting for 10 minutes, heat the remaining 2 tablespoons of oil in a large saucepan over high heat. Add onions and sauté for 1 minute. Reduce heat to medium and sauté for 5 to 6 minutes, or until onions have browned.

 Add garlic and sauté for 1 minute, until fragrant. Remove eggplant from the oven and add to the pan. Stir in cream (or coconut milk), making sure the vegetables are evenly coated. Pour in stock and maple syrup (or honey) and bring to a boil. Reduce heat to medium-low and simmer, uncovered, for 30 minutes. Turn stove off and purée mixture until smooth. Add lemon juice and season with salt and pepper.

Ladle soup into bowls and drizzle each serving with 1 teaspoon of mint oil. Enjoy!

mint oil

1 c mint leaves

¼ c extra-virgin olive oil

toasted cumin and eggplant soup

2 large eggplants, ends removed, peeled and cut into 1-inch cubes

¼ c olive oil (divided)

1 Tbsp cumin seeds

½ tsp crushed red pepper flakes

½ tsp kosher salt

2 large onions, coarsely chopped

11 cloves garlic, chopped

2 c whipping (33%) cream or coconut milk

1½ litres Vegetable Stock (p. 200)

2 Tbsp maple syrup or honey

juice of ½ lemon

kosher salt and ground black pepper, to taste

6 to 8 tsp Mint Oil (see here)

za'atar-roasted cauliflower, watercress and almond soup

serves 4 to 6

I started experimenting with za'atar after my trip to Israel, where I saw it used to season soups and finish meats. The Middle Eastern spice mixture is made of herbs, sesame seeds and salt and adds an aromatic fragrance to dishes. It shines most when used as a rub and roasted in the oven. Here, we keep the soup light with almond milk.

soup Preheat oven to 425°F. Line a baking sheet with parchment paper.

In a large bowl, combine cauliflower, za'atar, 2 tablespoons oil, lemon juice, salt and pepper and toss until florets are evenly coated. Transfer cauliflower onto the prepared baking sheet and bake for 10 to 12 minutes, or until golden crispy brown.

Meanwhile, in a medium saucepan over medium-high heat, sauté onions and garlic in 1 tablespoon oil for 3 to 4 minutes, until softened. Pour in stock and bring to a simmer.

Add cauliflower and almond milk to the pan and simmer for another 10 minutes to allow the roasted-cauliflower flavour to develop.

Transfer soup to a blender in batches (or use an immersion blender) and purée until smooth. Season to taste with salt, pepper, lemon juice and/or za'atar.

garnishes Preheat oven to 350°F.

Place almonds on a baking sheet and toast for 5 minutes, or until golden brown.

Ladle soup into bowls, then garnish each with watercress leaves and a tablespoon of toasted almonds. Finish with a drizzle of olive oil and serve!

soup

½ head large cauliflower, cut into 1-inch florets

2 Tbsp za'atar, plus extra to taste

3 Tbsp olive oil (divided)

juice of 1 lemon, plus extra to taste

kosher salt and ground black pepper, to taste

1 small white onion, chopped

2 cloves garlic, finely chopped

4 c Vegetable Stock (p. 200)

2 c unsweetened almond milk

garnishes

6 Tbsp slivered almonds

10 to 12 sprigs watercress, leaves only

extra-virgin olive oil, for drizzling

soups

the foundation

Stocks are the foundation of a lot of great cooking. Whether it's a soup, a sauce, a risotto or a stew, you're going to need a stock that's made with love. And by that, I mean a stock that is full of body and flavour. If you don't have a good stock, you won't have a good dish. It's as simple as that. And it's so easy to make that you won't look at commercial stock ever again.

Here are a few basics on making delicious stock:

Keep your trims and peels. The stuff a lot of home cooks throw away are the fundamentals of a good stock, so put those celery ends, carrot peels, onion skins, and meat and fish bones into the freezer and save them for stock-making day. Did you make a batch of fresh corn salsa? Save those corn cobs and make stock for corn soup.

Know how to time your stock. Have a general understanding of how long it takes to develop your flavours for different types of stock. A vegetable stock requires only forty-five minutes to an hour. A chicken stock will need between two to three hours simmering on the stove to pull all those flavours from the bones and to turn the colour of apple juice. Fish stock needs an hour and a half. And beef stock needs time: it can be a two-day affair. I've been known to simmer beef bones for three days.

Never boil. When making a protein stock, you are pulling impurities out of the bones, and you'll see those impurities rise to the surface. It's important to go slow and simmer and never, ever, boil your stock. Early on, a chef mentor taught me that if you boil your stock, it risks becoming cloudy and can even turn bitter. Ladle the fat or foam off the surface of your stock as it simmers. (I don't worry about skimming veggie stock.) Once cooked, strain your stock through a fine-mesh sieve.

Roast your bones. Before adding beef bones to your stock, be sure to roast them until they are golden brown. The process brings out the juices and melts down the marrow, so those bones are bursting with flavour. It takes about an hour in the oven at 400°F.

Enhance your stock. Add a mirepoix of celery and carrots to your stock as you cook it to add dimension to the flavour. But do not salt the stock—ever. Salt comes later, when making your final dish. And beware lemons that might remain in the roasted chicken carcass. Citrus should never make its way into a stock or the bitter pith will destroy the flavour. Also, starchy root veggies can turn a beautiful golden stock murky, so leave those out, too.

Cool it down. You can either use the stock immediately or cool it down to store for later use. At the restaurant, we put our big pot of stock into an ice bath in the sink and run cool water around the pot so it cools down quick. You can also freeze some in ice cube trays so you don't have to thaw an entire batch at once.

cioppino

4 tsp olive oil

⅓ c chopped onions

¼ bulb fennel, cored and chopped into bite-size pieces

4 tsp fennel seeds, toasted and crushed

1 clove garlic, finely chopped

pinch of crushed red pepper flakes

⅔ c white wine

1½ c canned whole tomatoes, crushed

1½ c clam nectar

4 sprigs thyme

1 bay leaf

8 mussels, scrubbed clean

8 clams, scrubbed clean

4 (21/25) prawns, peeled and deveined

2 squid, cleaned, halved and scored crisscross

4 oz ling cod or any thick white fish, divided into 4 pieces

kosher salt and ground black pepper, to taste

1½ Tbsp vegetable oil

juice of ½ lemon, plus extra to taste

2 Tbsp chopped Italian parsley

2 tsp chopped oregano

Cioppino is more of a meal than a soup, and this traditional Italian dish has many parts. It's all about technique: searing the fish, grilling the squid and steaming the mussels and clams. You need to be on your game for this one and pay close attention to your cooking times.

Heat olive oil in a large saucepan over medium heat. Add onions, fennel and fennel seeds and sauté for 30 seconds, ensuring the vegetables don't colour. (Reduce heat if needed.) Add garlic and red pepper flakes and sauté for another 2 minutes, lightly toasting without colouring.

Pour in wine and cook for another 2 to 3 minutes, until reduced by half. Add tomatoes, clam nectar, thyme and bay leaf. Reduce heat to low and simmer for 3 to 4 minutes to allow flavours to develop. Add mussels and clams, cover and steam for 4 to 5 minutes, until they have opened.

Season prawns, squid and fish with salt and pepper.

Heat vegetable oil in a medium frying pan over high heat, until just smoking. Add fish and sear one side for 1 minute, until nicely browned. Flip over and turn the heat off. Add prawns and squid to the pan and cook for 1 minute, or until colour begins to change. Flip over squid and prawns and cook for another minute, until cooked through. Pour lemon juice over mixture. Carefully transfer mixture into the pan with mussels and clams.

Season to taste with salt, pepper and lemon juice. Remove thyme sprigs and bay leaf, then garnish with parsley and oregano.

lobster cauliflower soup

lobster stock

shells from 6 small lobsters

2 leeks, white and light green
parts, roughly chopped

1 stalk celery, roughly chopped

2 large carrots, roughly
chopped

1 bulb garlic, halved

bunch of thyme

3 bay leaves

2 Tbsp tomato paste

lobster cauliflower soup

3 Tbsp olive oil

1 large onion, roughly chopped

1 large leek, white part only,
sliced

1 stalk celery, sliced

4 cloves garlic, finely chopped

3 sprigs thyme

2 bay leaves

2 c white wine

1 head cauliflower, cored and
roughly chopped

½ large Yukon Gold potato,
roughly chopped

2 tsp tomato paste

2 c whipping (33%) cream

2 litres Lobster Stock (see here)

2 tsp maple syrup

lemon juice, to taste

cayenne pepper, to taste

kosher salt and ground black
pepper, to taste

Every soup starts with a great stock, and here we use a stock made with lobster shells. (Ask your fishmonger for them.) If you want to go dairy-free, you can sub the cream for cashew or almond milk. It's a versatile soup that's just a little decadent.

lobster stock Preheat oven to 400°F.

Put lobster shells on a baking sheet and roast for 30 to 35 minutes, or until dried. Using a mallet or heavy-bottomed saucepan, crush lobster shells until broken up.

Combine all ingredients in a stockpot and add 6 litres water. Bring to a boil, then reduce heat and simmer for 45 minutes to 1 hour. Strain and discard the solids. The stock can be stored in an airtight container in the refrigerator for 3 days. Or freeze until needed.

lobster cauliflower soup Heat oil in a large saucepan over medium heat. Add onions and sauté for 45 seconds. Add leeks and celery and sauté for another 30 seconds. Add garlic, thyme and bay leaves and sauté for 2 minutes.

Pour in white wine and cook for another 2 to 3 minutes, until liquid has reduced by half. Add cauliflower, potatoes and tomato paste and stir until all ingredients are coated with tomato paste. Pour in cream and bring to a boil.

Pour in lobster stock and maple syrup and simmer, uncovered, for 45 minutes. Transfer soup to a blender and blend until smooth. Season to taste with lemon juice, cayenne, salt and pepper. Serve.

serves 4 **barley, kale and soppressata soup**

This is a great winter soup, hearty and delicious. Soppressata is an Italian salami that has been dry-cured for months, but you could easily swap it out for prosciutto, pancetta or chorizo if you like. Or you can make the soup vegetarian by leaving out the soppressata.

Place barley in a saucepan of water, bring to a boil and reduce to a simmer. Simmer for 1½ hours. Drain and set aside.

Heat oil in a medium saucepan over medium heat. Add soppressata and sauté for 30 seconds. Add onions and sauté for another minute. Add garlic and red peppers and sauté for 1 minute.

Pour in wine to deglaze the pan and cook for 1 minute, until liquid is reduced by half. Add tomato purée and stock. Bring to a boil, reduce heat to medium-low and simmer for 10 minutes.

Add barley, cover and simmer for another 5 minutes. Turn off the heat and add kale, zucchini and lemon zest and juice. Season to taste with salt and pepper. Portion into bowls and serve!

½ c pearled barley

1 Tbsp olive oil

8 oz soppressata salami, cut into a ½-inch dice

½ small red onion, finely chopped

2 cloves garlic, finely chopped

¼ c chopped red bell pepper

½ c white wine

1 c tomato purée

4 c Vegetable Stock (p. 200)

2 c loosely packed black kale, stems removed and thinly sliced

½ small zucchini, cut into a ½-inch dice

grated zest and juice of 1 small lemon

kosher salt and ground black pepper, to taste

serves 6   Thai red curry coconut duck soup

We order the barbecue duck from the pros who make it in Chinatown. But you could use roasted chicken or leftover steak, or even keep the soup vegetarian. This dish includes a homemade red curry paste, which is so much better than anything in the jar. Make double and use it in our Coconut-Lemongrass Braised Beef Short Ribs (p. 139).

Peking duck stock   In a stockpot, combine all ingredients and add 5 litres water. (Reserve meat for later use.) Bring to a boil, reduce heat to medium and simmer for 1½ hours. Strain stock and store in containers. It can be refrigerated for 3 days or frozen for up to 3 months.

Thai red curry coconut duck soup   Combine oil, sugar and curry paste in a large saucepan and stir over medium heat, until sugar has dissolved.

Pour in stock and fish sauce and bring to a boil. Add lime leaves, lemongrass and galangal (or ginger) and bring back to a boil. Reduce heat to medium-low and simmer for 10 to 15 minutes.

Strain liquid into a separate saucepan and keep warm over medium heat. Add coconut milk, red onions, bell peppers, mushrooms, carrots, corn, lime juice and duck meat and bring to a boil. Reduce heat to medium-low and simmer 12 to 15 minutes. Remove from heat, then stir in green onions, snap peas and Thai basil. Ladle into bowls and serve.

Peking duck stock

1 whole Peking duck, bones only, meat reserved

1 red onion, roughly chopped

1 carrot, roughly chopped

6 green onions, roughly chopped

¼ c roughly chopped ginger

1 bulb garlic, unpeeled and halved

Thai red curry coconut duck soup

3 Tbsp vegetable oil

6 Tbsp palm sugar

¼ c Red Curry Paste (p. 199)

3½ litres Peking Duck Stock (see here)

5 Tbsp fish sauce

8 kaffir lime leaves

2 stalks lemongrass, outer two layers discarded, chopped

½ c chopped galangal or ginger

4 c coconut milk

½ red onion, thinly sliced

1 red bell pepper, seeded, deveined and cut into thin strips

1 c enoki mushrooms

1 c shimeji mushrooms

1 carrot, cut into thin strips

1 c corn kernels

¼ c fresh lime juice

2 c reserved Peking duck meat, skin-on, sliced into bite-size pieces

3 green onions, chopped

1 c snap peas, cut into thin strips

1 c Thai basil leaves

Moroccan lamb, tomato and chickpea soup

serves 4 to 6

ras el hanout

1 tsp ground cumin

1 tsp ground ginger

1 tsp ground cardamom

1 tsp kosher salt

1 tsp ground black pepper

½ tsp ground cinnamon

½ tsp ground coriander

½ tsp cayenne pepper

½ tsp allspice

¼ tsp ground cloves

Moroccan lamb, tomato and chickpea soup

1 Tbsp vegetable oil

½ lb lamb shoulder, cut into ¼-inch pieces

½ small red onion, thinly sliced

1 (1-inch) piece ginger, peeled and grated

4 cloves garlic, finely chopped

1 tsp harissa powder

1 tsp Ras El Hanout (see here)

½ tsp toasted cumin seeds

½ tsp toasted fennel seeds

½ tsp ground black pepper

½ tsp ground coriander

½ tsp ground turmeric

1 (2-inch) cinnamon stick

1 c tomato purée

4 c Vegetable Stock (p. 200)

½ c chopped carrots

½ preserved lemon (store-bought), chopped

½ tsp dried mint

1 c cooked Chickpeas (p. 198)

2 c loosely packed spinach

kosher salt and ground black pepper

This North African–style soup becomes more flavourful the longer it cooks. And toasting the spices elevates that gorgeous flavour. If you reduce the liquid, it becomes a nourishing one-pot main that can be served with rice.

ras el hanout Combine all ingredients in an airtight container and use when needed.

Moroccan lamb, tomato and chickpea soup Heat oil in a large saucepan over medium heat. Add lamb and sear for 2 minutes in total. Using a slotted spoon, transfer lamb to a plate and set aside. Keep the fat in the pan, add onion and sauté for 2 minutes.

Add ginger and garlic and sauté for another minute. Reduce heat to low, then add harissa, ras el hanout, cumin seeds, fennel seeds, black pepper, coriander, turmeric and cinnamon stick. Sauté for a minute, until fragrant.

Add tomato purée and stock. Bring to a boil, then add reserved lamb, carrots, preserved lemon and dried mint. Cover with a lid and simmer for 30 to 45 minutes to develop the flavours.

Turn off the heat and stir in chickpeas and spinach. Remove the cinnamon stick and season to taste with salt and pepper. Ladle into bowls and serve!

vegetarian

pan-seared halloumi cheese and caramelized fennel with orange-pomegranate reduction

serves 4

Halloumi is a salty Middle Eastern cheese that handles heat well. Pomegranate molasses (which is essentially reduced pomegranate juice) can be found in any specialty shop—it's a versatile condiment that you'll want to add to your pantry.

deep-fried pita chips Heat oil in a large saucepan to a temperature of 350°F. (Use a thermometer for an accurate reading.)

Using a 1¼-inch ring cutter, cut out rounds from pitas. Carefully lower pita rounds into the oil and deep-fry for 45 seconds, or until pita turns golden brown. Transfer to a paper towel–lined tray.

halloumi cheese and caramelized fennel Put cheese in a bowl of cold water and soak for at least 1 hour.

Preheat the oven to 450°F. With a small knife, carefully segment both oranges and set aside. Squeeze out all possible juice from the leftover membranes of the oranges into a small bowl.

In a bowl, toss fennel with maple syrup, vinegar and oil and season with salt and pepper. Arrange fennel on a roasting pan and roast for 20 to 25 minutes, or until the fennel is golden brown and caramelized. Drizzle with pomegranate molasses and reserved orange juice and toss lightly until the fennel is evenly coated. Bake for another 10 minutes.

Pat halloumi dry with a paper towel.

Heat oil in a frying pan over high heat. Gently place halloumi into pan and sear for 15 seconds, until golden brown. Flip over and cook for another 15 seconds.

Scatter watercress on a serving platter, then top with pan-seared halloumi, roasted fennel, orange segments and deep-fried pita chips.

deep-fried pita chips

6 c canola oil

4 pitas

halloumi cheese and caramelized fennel

12 oz halloumi cheese, cut into ½-inch-thick slices

2 oranges

4 bulbs fennel, cored and cut into 1-inch-thick slices

½ c maple syrup

¼ c sherry vinegar

3 Tbsp extra-virgin olive oil

2 Tbsp pomegranate molasses

kosher salt and ground black pepper, to taste

1 Tbsp vegetable oil, for frying

1 bunch watercress, harder stems removed

16 Deep-Fried Pita Chips (see here)

grilled corn and tomato succotash with arugula chimichurri

arugula chimichurri

½ bunch cilantro, coarsely chopped

1 c tightly packed arugula, coarsely chopped

4 cloves garlic, finely chopped

1 tsp crushed red pepper flakes

½ tsp cumin seeds, crushed

½ tsp kosher salt, plus extra to taste

½ c extra-virgin olive oil

¼ c red wine vinegar

ground black pepper, to taste

grilled corn and tomato succotash

2 cobs corn

2 Tbsp extra-virgin olive oil

2 shallots, chopped

2 cloves garlic, finely chopped

12 grape tomatoes, halved

½ c fava beans, blanched and peeled

1½ Tbsp finely chopped jalapeño

3 Tbsp apple cider vinegar

16 basil leaves, cut into thin strips

kosher salt and ground black pepper, to taste

grilled bread

1 (12-inch) baguette, halved lengthwise

2 Tbsp extra-virgin olive oil

sea salt and ground black pepper, to taste

This dish is a mash-up of traditions: a down-home American side dish of corn and fava beans, and a South American condiment that often accompanies meat. Here, in the chimichurri, we swap out the traditionally used parsley with peppery arugula.

arugula chimichurri In a food processor, combine all ingredients and process until smooth. Season with salt and pepper to taste. Set aside at room temperature.

grilled corn and tomato succotash Bring a large saucepan of salted water to a boil. Add corn and simmer for 3 to 4 minutes. Drain and set side.

Preheat grill over high heat to 400°F.

Place corn onto the hot grill and lightly char. Set aside to cool, then carefully cut off kernels. Set aside.

Heat oil in a frying pan over medium heat. Add shallots and sauté for 2 to 3 minutes, until translucent. (Careful not to burn.) Add garlic and sauté for another minute, until fragrant. Stir in tomatoes, corn, fava beans and jalapeños and sauté for 2 minutes, stirring occasionally. (Be careful not to overcook.) Add vinegar. Remove from heat, then stir in basil. Season to taste with salt and pepper. Set succotash aside.

grilled bread Preheat grill over high heat to 400°F.

Brush oil on each piece of baguette, then season with salt and pepper. Grill both sides, then cut them in half widthwise.

assembly Fold the chimichurri into the succotash. Taste and season if needed. Spread a generous amount onto the grilled bread and serve.

glorious veggies

As a chef, there's never been a more exciting, creative time in the world of plant-based cuisine. It used to be that the vegetable was a mere afterthought, the mashed potato or the dutifully steamed broccoli tucked to the side of the plate. In the nineties, baby vegetables were the rage, which was about as creative as it got—until recently. Now, there's an explosion of options, thanks to the growth of organic farming and the farm-to-table movement, which have brought us an infusion of previously unseen products: heirloom tomatoes, purple potatoes, brown pears, rainbow coloured carrots, hardneck garlic, daikon, celeriac, Jerusalem artichokes, kohlrabi, Japanese eggplants and Romanesco (a fancy cauliflower). It sure beats the days when I was a kid and iceberg lettuce and English cucumbers ruled the produce section. Today's kids get to cook with salsify and heirloom radishes.

There's a heightened dietary awareness in today's food scene, and chefs have taken note. At the Dirty Apron, we've made a point of offering plant-based and gluten-free options to our customers, which is a must in this era of conscientious food choices. Vancouver is an outdoorsy, active city, and many of my health-conscious customers look out for the brightly coloured, vitamin-rich salads and smoothies we now sell at our deli. I've even ratcheted up the fruit and veg in my own diet, and when cooking for family.

Plant-based diets have become increasingly popular with the under-thirty-five demographic, in particular. A poll conducted by Dalhousie University showed that a little more than 7 per cent of Canadians consider themselves vegetarians and 2.3 per cent vegan. And people under thirty-five are three times more likely to fall in the meat-free camp than people older than forty-nine.

And while plant-based diets are a way of life for the younger generation, they're also gaining traction with anyone who wants a healthier lifestyle or cleaner planet. We all know that obesity is on the rise, and diet-related illnesses, such as diabetes, are increasingly facts of life. That's why so many vegetarian restaurants are flourishing in major cities throughout North America and Europe, and why Canadian consumption of most red meat and pork has been falling for the last decade, according to Statistics Canada.

Everything I do comes back to flavour. So when it comes to cooking plant-based foods, the principles aren't much different than cooking with meat. It's about pulling out as much flavour as possible, whether that's through cooking techniques or adding a little sweetness, spice, acid or texture. The key, of course, is not to overcook your veg. (We kill flavour by overcooking the chlorophylls in vegetables.) Overcooked Brussels sprouts can turn a kid off veg for a lifetime. Trust me, I would know.

Know your product, its water content, and how naturally sweet or starchy it is. The easiest way to coax flavour out of a veg is to grill, roast or pan-sear it to caramelize the sugars, which are instant flavour bombs. And of course, deep-frying a veg adds not just crunch, but also flavour. You want to layer those textures and balance those flavours in a dish. So take notice of the sweetness of roasted carrots, the crispiness of baked or fried kale, the richness of cashews and the umami flavour of miso or eggplant, and up your plant-based cooking game to something with variety and complexity. And next time you're at the farmers' market, explore the bounty of new products and try cooking with something outside your comfort zone.

kale and zucchini spaetzle with toasted pumpkin seeds and shaved pecorino

serves 4

spaetzle

4 large eggs

1 c milk

2 c all-purpose flour

kosher salt and ground black pepper, to taste

extra-virgin olive oil, to coat

assembly

1 small zucchini, thinly sliced

1 bunch green kale, stems removed and cut into bite-size pieces

½ bunch purple kale, stems removed and cut into bite-size pieces

1½ Tbsp extra-virgin olive oil

kosher salt and ground black pepper, to taste

grated zest and juice of 2 lemons, plus extra to taste

6 Tbsp unsalted butter

3 c cooked Spaetzle (see here)

¼ c shelled pumpkin seeds, toasted

¼ c chopped Italian parsley, for garnish

2 oz pecorino cheese, shaved, for garnish

I travel to Germany frequently to visit my in-laws, so I've learned a lot about German cuisine. Spaetzle is their pasta, basically, but a lot easier to make. Be sure to toast the pumpkin seeds for crunch and use good pecorino cheese. If you go to a good, well-stocked specialty store, you can find imported sheep's milk pecorino—which is superior to the cow's milk version you'll find at supermarkets.

spaetzle In a bowl, whisk eggs and milk together.

In a separate bowl, combine flour, salt and pepper. Make a well in the centre of the dry ingredients and pour in the egg-milk mixture. Gradually draw in flour from the sides and combine, until dough is smooth and thick. Set aside for 5 minutes to rest.

Bring a large saucepan of salted water to a boil, reduce heat to medium and maintain a simmer.

Using a spatula, push the dough through the holes of a colander into the simmering water, working in batches to avoid overcrowding. Cook for 1 to 2 minutes, stirring gently, until spaetzle floats to the surface. Transfer spaetzle into a colander and quickly rinse under cold running water, then put it in a bowl. Repeat until all of the spaetzle have been cooked. Add a little oil and toss to lightly coat.

assembly Preheat grill over high heat to 400°F.

Place zucchini and kale into a bowl and season with oil, salt and pepper.

Carefully place zucchini and kale on the hot grill and grill for 2 minutes, or until kale becomes crispy and is lightly charred. (Purple kale tends to char, but not get crispy.)

Transfer zucchini and kale to a bowl. Add lemon zest and juice and set aside.

Heat butter in a large frying pan over high heat, until it begins to crackle and pop and brown at the edges of the pan. Immediately turn off heat and stir in spaetzle. Add zucchini, kale and pumpkin seeds and lightly toss together. Season to taste with salt, pepper and/or more lemon zest and juice.

Transfer to a serving platter and garnish with parsley and pecorino.

tomato-sorrel risotto with garlic confit

serves 4

When I create a creamy-textured dish like risotto, I like the contrasting punch of acidity. Remember, it's all about a balance of flavour. Here, you get the tang of sorrel, tomato and white wine, rounded out by the garlic confit and Parmesan.

In a medium saucepan, combine stock and puréed tomatoes and heat through over medium heat. Keep hot.

Heat oil in a separate saucepan over medium heat. Add shallots and garlic and cook for 2 minutes. (Do not allow them to colour.) Add rice, increase heat to medium-high and stir for 1 minute.

Pour in wine and continue to stir until all the wine has been absorbed into the rice. Add a ladle of hot stock and a pinch of salt. Reduce heat to medium-low and simmer so the rice doesn't cook too quickly. Add another ladle of stock and stir until it's been absorbed into the rice. Repeat for 15 minutes, or until rice is soft but with a slight bite.

Remove from the heat and stir in butter, Roma tomatoes, Parmesan, parsley and sorrel. Season with salt and pepper.

Garnish with freshly grated Parmesan and garlic confit. Drizzle garlic confit olive oil overtop and serve.

4 c Vegetable Stock (p. 200)

2 c puréed tomatoes

2 Tbsp olive oil

4 shallots, finely chopped

4 cloves garlic, finely chopped

1⅓ c carnaroli or Arborio rice

⅔ c dry white wine

kosher salt, to taste

¼ c (½ stick) unsalted butter

4 Roma tomatoes, seeded and diced

1 c grated Parmesan cheese, plus extra for garnishing

¼ c chopped Italian parsley

½ c chopped sorrel

ground black pepper, to taste

½ cup Garlic Confit (p. 198), for garnish

¼ cup Garlic Confit olive oil (p. 198), for garnish

serves 4   quinoa nourish bowl

This is fun and playful good-for-you food without rules. Sub out the vegetables of your choice and hit it with a bit of Sriracha, or any kind of hot sauce.

deep-fried quinoa   Place quinoa in a bowl and rinse with cold water. Drain and repeat until water runs clear. Drain quinoa.

In a small saucepan, combine quinoa, salt and 3 cups water. Bring to a light simmer over medium heat, then reduce heat to low. Cover and cook for 15 minutes. Turn off heat and set aside, covered, for another 15 minutes.

Heat oil in a deep fryer or deep saucepan to a temperature of 350°F. (Use a thermometer for an accurate reading.) Line a baking sheet with paper towels and have a small fine-mesh sieve on hand.

Carefully lower 2 cups cooked quinoa into oil and deep-fry for 2 minutes, until golden brown and crunchy. Reserve the rest of the cooked quinoa. Using the sieve, transfer deep-fried quinoa to the prepared baking sheet. Season with salt and pepper. Set aside.

nourish bowl   Heat oil in a frying pan over medium-high heat. Add zucchini and asparagus and cook, untouched, for 3 to 4 minutes, until browned. Flip over, then add garlic and leeks. Season with salt and pepper and sauté for 1 minute. Stir in cooked quinoa, carefully folding into the sautéed vegetables. Turn off heat.

Add Swiss chard, green onions, parsley, sorrel, soy sauce, and lemon juice and fold in. Season with salt and pepper.

Add 1 cup deep-fried quinoa and the seeds.

Serve in individual bowls or family style. Garnish with radishes and the remaining 1 cup deep-fried quinoa.

deep-fried quinoa

2 c quinoa

2 tsp kosher salt, plus extra to taste

4 c canola oil

ground black pepper, to taste

nourish bowl

2 Tbsp extra-virgin olive oil

1 zucchini, thinly sliced

8 asparagus spears, ends trimmed, halved lengthwise

2 cloves garlic, thinly sliced

½ leek, white part only, cut into ¼-inch-thick rounds

kosher salt and ground black pepper, to taste

2 c reserved cooked quinoa

4 leaves Swiss chard, finely torn

4 green onions, chopped

2 Tbsp chopped Italian parsley

1 c loosely packed sorrel, chopped

3 Tbsp soy sauce

juice of 2 lemons

2 c Deep-Fried Quinoa (see here)

¼ c shelled pumpkin seeds, toasted

¼ c sunflower seeds, toasted

8 radishes, thinly sliced

miso-sake roasted Japanese eggplant

**miso-sake roasted
Japanese eggplant**

6 Tbsp sake

6 Tbsp mirin

1 c white miso

½ c + 2 Tbsp granulated sugar

4 Japanese eggplants

green onions, cut into thin
strips, for garnish

sesame rice cakes

2 c Japanese short-grain rice

¼ c toasted sesame seeds

2 Tbsp vegetable oil, for frying

In our first book, we brought you Miso-Sake Roasted Sablefish, and now we bring you the equally delicious eggplant version. I love the way this crowd-pleasing dish comes together on the plate. Serve it with something crispy as a side, such as Broccolini and Snap Pea Salad with Tahini-Soy Dressing (p. 43).

miso-sake roasted Japanese eggplant In a small saucepan, combine sake and mirin and bring to a boil. Cook for 20 seconds until all the alcohol is burnt off. (Be careful as alcohol may flame.) Turn heat off and whisk in miso until smooth. Add sugar and bring back to a boil over high heat. Remove from heat and stir continuously to prevent the marinade from burning. Set aside to cool.

Cut eggplants in half lengthwise and remove stem, then cut widthwise into 4 pieces. Using the tip of the knife, cut an incision along the centre of each half, making sure not to cut through the skin. Put the eggplant in a baking dish and pour in marinade. Mix and refrigerate for at least 2 hours or up to 2 days.

Preheat oven to 475°F. Line a baking sheet with aluminum foil.

Place eggplant on the prepared baking sheet and bake for 12 minutes. Be careful not to burn and check regularly. If the eggplant is not fully cooked, but is fully caramelized, turn the oven off completely and allow to cook in residual heat until tender. Set aside.

sesame rice cakes Place rice in a bowl and rinse with cold water. Drain and repeat until water runs clear. Drain rice.

Combine rice and 2½ cups water in a rice cooker and set to cook. (Alternatively, combine rice and water in a saucepan and cover with a lid. Bring to a boil, then reduce heat to low and simmer for 12 minutes. Do not remove the lid! Turn off heat and set pan aside, covered, for another 10 minutes.) Transfer rice to a bowl and carefully break it apart with a wet wooden spoon. Stir in sesame seeds.

Fill a bowl with cold water. (Dipping your hands in the water will make the rice easier to handle.) On a cutting board, fill a 2- or 3-inch ring cutter with rice and pat to a ½-inch thickness. Set aside and repeat with remaining rice.

Heat oil in a frying pan over high heat. Add rice cakes and cook for 2 to 3 minutes on each side, until golden brown and edges crisp. Keep warm in the oven until needed.

assembly Place eggplant on top of the crispy rice cakes and garnish with green onions.

creamy orzo with roasted portobello mushrooms and sherry-maple caramelized onions

serves 4

roasted mushrooms

4 large portobello mushrooms, stems removed

¼ c extra-virgin olive oil

kosher salt and ground black pepper, to taste

roasted sweet onions

2 Tbsp vegetable oil

2 small onions, halved

4 tsp maple syrup

4 tsp unsalted butter

2 tsp sherry vinegar

creamy orzo

½ c heavy (36%) cream

2 c cooked orzo

½ c Asiago cheese

4 tsp finely chopped rosemary

¼ c finely chopped Italian parsley

kosher salt and ground black pepper, to taste

Although this little pasta looks more like rice, the translation of the Italian word orzo is "barley." Orzo is delicious bowl food, especially when combined with a creamy sauce, and this dish is perfect for a cool day when you crave something filling and hearty.

roasted mushrooms Preheat oven to 450°F. Line a baking sheet with aluminum foil.

In a small bowl, combine mushrooms, oil, salt and pepper and toss. Transfer to the prepared baking sheet and roast for 10 minutes. Keep warm.

roasted sweet onions Preheat oven to 400°F.

Heat oil in a small ovenproof frying pan over high heat. Add onions, flat-side down, and sear untouched for 2 minutes, until caramelized. Transfer pan to the oven and roast for 20 minutes, until onions are soft and tender.

Pour in maple syrup, butter and vinegar and cook over low heat for 3 to 4 minutes, until onions absorb the liquid and are sticky. Keep warm.

creamy orzo Bring cream to a boil in a medium saucepan, then reduce heat to medium-low and simmer. Stir in orzo, Asiago and rosemary and simmer until it has a creamy consistency. Stir in parsley and season with salt and pepper. Set aside.

assembly Serve family-style with orzo, onions and mushroom in separate serving dishes.

barley, wild rice and farro cabbage rolls with tomato-fennel sauce

serves 4

tomato sauce

1 Tbsp olive oil

½ large onion, chopped

5 cloves garlic, finely chopped

5 c canned whole tomatoes

10 basil leaves

½ Tbsp kosher salt

½ Tbsp ground black pepper

½ tsp crushed red pepper flakes

hummus

1¼ c dried chickpeas, soaked in 5 c water overnight

¼ c extra-virgin olive oil

¼ c tahini

2 cloves garlic

1 Tbsp kosher salt, plus extra to taste

1½ tsp cumin seeds

1 tsp crushed red pepper flakes

1 tsp dried mint

juice of 2½ lemons

ground black pepper, to taste

continued facing

Golabki is a traditional hearty Polish dish that is commonly served at festive occasions. It's anything wrapped in cabbage leaves, and here we've packed them with superfoods—chewy barley, nutty wild rice and farro wheat—for texture. If you want gluten-free cabbage rolls, simply omit the farro.

tomato sauce Heat oil in a large saucepan over medium heat. Add onions and sauté for 2 to 3 minutes. Add garlic and sauté for another minute. Stir in tomatoes and bring to a boil, then reduce heat to medium-low and simmer for 30 minutes. Turn heat off.

Stir in basil, salt, pepper and red pepper flakes. Using an immersion blender, purée until smooth. (Makes about 1½ litres of sauce. Any leftover sauce can be stored in the freezer for up to 1 month.)

hummus In a saucepan, combine chickpeas and soaking water and cook over high heat for 2½ hours, or until tender. Drain chickpeas.

In a blender, combine chickpeas, oil, tahini, garlic, salt, cumin seeds, red pepper flakes, mint and lemon juice and purée until smooth. Season to taste with salt and pepper.

vegetarian

cabbage rolls Place barley, farro and wild rice in 3 separate saucepans. Fill each pan with water, bring to a boil and reduce to a simmer. Simmer for 1 hour. Drain and set aside.

Preheat oven to 400°F. Fill a large bowl with ice water.

In a medium bowl, combine grains, onions, fennel, sun-dried tomatoes, herbs, hummus and vinegar.

Bring a medium saucepan of salted water to a boil. Remove 8 outer layers of the cabbage. Add those leaves to the pan and blanch for 20 seconds. Drain, then immediately plunge them in the ice bath to cool. Drain.

Carefully remove outer rib of cabbage leaves while keeping the leaves intact and whole.

Portion filling into the cabbage leaves. Starting from the bottom of the leaf, roll bottom to the centre, folding sides to centre to making sure everything is contained. Gently pull folded area of the leaf down and flip leaf so that a small bundle has been formed.

Pour tomato sauce into a casserole dish, then arrange cabbage rolls on top. Drizzle with oil and bake for 20 minutes. Serve family-style.

cabbage rolls

½ c pearled barley

½ c farro

½ c wild rice

1 small onion, finely chopped

½ small bulb fennel, cored and finely chopped

10 sun-dried tomatoes, sliced

2 Tbsp chopped Italian parsley

2 sprigs rosemary, leaves only, chopped

2 sprigs thyme, leaves only

⅔ c Hummus (see here)

2 Tbsp sherry vinegar

1 Savoy cabbage

2 c Tomato Sauce (see here)

extra-virgin olive oil, for drizzling

lemon-ricotta gnudi with crispy basil

Gnudi is gnocchi's plump cousin. These airy, cloud-like dumplings are delicate because they're made with ricotta, and the fried basil adds a little crunch to the dish. Finish with a few shavings of quality Parmesan and you've got heaven in a bowl.

lemon-ricotta gnudi Combine ricotta, pecorino, eggs, lemon zest, salt and pepper in a food processor, and mix until smooth. Transfer to a bowl and add flour. Using a spoon, gently combine until evenly mixed.

Lightly flour a clean work surface. Generously coat the dough with the flour, then use your hands to roll out a long rope, about ½ inch in diameter. Cut into 1-inch pieces and roll into individual balls.

Bring a large saucepan of salted water to a boil. Add gnudi and cook for 4 minutes, until they float to the surface. Transfer to a baking sheet lined with paper towels and drizzle with oil.

crispy basil Heat enough oil to coat the bottom of a large frying pan over medium heat. Add basil and fry for 1 minute. Turn and fry for another minute, until crispy. (Careful not to burn.) Transfer basil to a paper towel–lined plate.

In the same frying pan over high heat, cook gnudi on one side for 1 minute, until golden. Flip over, then add butter to the pan and cook for another minute. (If gnudi is dry, add 1 to 2 tablespoons of extra butter to coat.) Season with salt and pepper to taste.

Turn heat off and stir in vincotto (or balsamic vinegar).

confit tomatoes Preheat oven to 375°F.

In a small ovenproof casserole dish or deep skillet, combine tomatoes, garlic, bay leaves and thyme. Pour in oil to cover and bake for 7 to 10 minutes, or until tomatoes begin to pop. Remove from the oven and set aside.

assembly Spoon gnudi onto a large serving platter, then arrange the crispy basil on top. Spoon confit around the gnudi and scatter shaved Parmesan on top.

lemon-ricotta gnudi

1 lb ricotta cheese

¼ c pecorino cheese

2 large eggs

grated zest of 2 lemons

kosher salt and ground black pepper, to taste

½ c Italian "00" flour, plus extra for dusting

extra-virgin olive oil, for drizzling

shaved Parmesan cheese, to serve

crispy basil

olive oil, for frying

12 basil leaves

¼ c (½ stick) unsalted butter, plus extra if needed

2 Tbsp vincotto or aged balsamic vinegar

kosher salt and ground black pepper, to taste

confit tomatoes

1 pint cherry tomatoes (about 25)

3 cloves garlic

2 bay leaves

1 sprig thyme

2 c olive oil

roasted squash and pine nut tortellini with wild mushroom ragout

serves 4
(or 6 small plates)

pasta dough

1 c Italian "00" flour, plus extra for dusting

1 c semola flour (see Chef's Note)

4 large eggs

1 Tbsp extra-virgin olive oil

butternut squash tortellini

1 butternut squash, about 3½ lbs, peeled, seeded and cut into 2½-inch pieces

2 Tbsp extra-virgin olive oil

kosher salt and ground black pepper, to taste

1 c finely grated Parmesan cheese

¾ c toasted pine nuts

1 Tbsp chopped sage

ground nutmeg, to taste

truffle oil, to taste

continued facing

Italian "00" flour is finely ground and commonly used for pasta. Here, we combine it with semola flour, which is a durum wheat flour. Be careful not to overfill your tortellini, or they will burst during cooking.

pasta dough In a large bowl, combine flours and mix well. Make a well in the centre.

Crack eggs into the centre and add oil. Using a fork, beat the eggs and oil until smooth. Mix together with the flour. Transfer the dough to a lightly floured surface and use your hands to knead until the dough becomes smooth, silky and elastic. Wrap the dough in plastic wrap and set aside for 15 minutes before rolling or shaping. (You can wrap and store the dough at this point. Wrap the dough well in plastic wrap and refrigerate for up to 3 days.)

To roll the pasta, lightly flour the work surface and pasta machine. Set the rollers at the widest setting, then work half the dough through the rollers. Fold the dough over itself and work through the rollers again. Repeat until the dough feels like suede. Repeat with the other half of the dough.

Adjust the knob to the next narrowest setting and pass through the rollers again. Continue to pass the dough through the rollers, setting the machine down another notch after each roll. If the dough becomes too long to handle, cut it in half.

Roll the dough down to the last or second-to-last notch.

butternut squash tortellini Preheat oven to 400°F.

In a large bowl, toss squash in oil and season with salt and pepper. Place on a baking sheet and bake for 40 minutes, until tender.

Carefully transfer the hot squash to a food processor and blend until smooth. Remove squash and set aside in a bowl to cool.

Stir in Parmesan, pine nuts, sage, nutmeg and truffle oil and season to taste with salt and pepper.

vegetarian

filling tortellini Cut out rounds from the rolled pasta with a 3-inch cutter. Brush the rounds with water. Place one teaspoon of filling just off-centre on the circle of dough and fold the top flap of dough over it, creating a half moon shape. Press the edges with your thumb and forefinger to gently seal the pasta. Twist the two ends of the pasta together around your finger and seal together. Set aside.

wild mushroom ragout Heat oil and butter in a frying pan over medium-high heat, until butter melts and starts to foam. Add shallots and garlic and cook for 1 minute, until fragrant. Add mushrooms and cook for 3 to 4 minutes, stirring frequently.

Pour in stock and cook until liquid has reduced and thickened. Stir in tomatoes, herbs, truffle oil, salt and pepper. Reduce heat to low while you cook your pasta.

assembly Bring a saucepan of salted water to a boil. Carefully lower tortellini into the pan and cook for 2 to 3 minutes, until tender. Drain, then add tortellini to the pan with the mushrooms and toss. Transfer to individual plates and garnish each dish with freshly grated Parmesan and a drizzle of oil.

wild mushroom ragout

1 Tbsp extra-virgin olive oil

2 Tbsp unsalted butter

4 shallots, finely chopped

4 cloves garlic, finely chopped

2 lbs wild mushrooms, cleaned and larger mushrooms chopped

2 c Vegetable Stock (p. 200)

2 Roma tomatoes, seeded and cut into a ¼-inch dice

1 Tbsp basil leaves, chopped

1 Tbsp chopped Italian parsley

2 tsp thyme leaves

2 tsp oregano leaves

truffle oil, to taste

kosher salt and ground black pepper, to taste

assembly

grated Parmesan cheese

extra-virgin olive oil, for drizzling

CHEF'S NOTE
Semolina and semola are not actually the same thing. Semolina is a coarsely ground durum wheat, which resembles cornmeal more than flour. The Italian semola is also durum wheat, but very finely ground durum. We use the latter at the school and throughout the book.

butternut squash and ricotta gnocchi

butternut squash and ricotta gnocchi

1 butternut squash
½ c vegetable oil, for brushing
1 c ricotta, drained
¾ c grated Parmesan cheese
1 tsp freshly grated nutmeg
kosher salt and ground black pepper, to taste
1⅓ c all-purpose flour, plus extra for dusting

assembly

2 Tbsp unsalted butter
1 Tbsp extra-virgin olive oil
3 Tbsp torn basil leaves
2 Tbsp shaved Parmesan

We make gnocchi at our cooking school, and rarely does anyone get it wrong, because it's so easy. It's a dough that doesn't want any kneading—in fact, the less, the better. You won't miss the protein eating this dish because it's so stick-to-the-ribs satisfying.

butternut squash and ricotta gnocchi Preheat oven to 375°F.

Cut the squash in half lengthwise and remove the seeds. Lightly brush each half with oil and place flesh-side down on a baking sheet. Roast the squash for 1 hour, or until tender. Set aside to cool slightly, then scoop out the flesh. Discard the skin.

Put the squash in a food processor and purée until smooth. Measure 2 packed cups of squash purée and refrigerate until chilled.

In a large bowl, combine squash, ricotta, Parmesan, nutmeg, salt and pepper and mix well. Gradually fold in flour, making sure not to overwork the dough.

Dredge the dough with flour, then roll out by hand into a rope with a ¾-inch diameter. Cut the rope into 1-inch pieces and place on a lightly floured baking sheet.

Bring a large saucepan of salted water to a boil. Carefully lower gnocchi into the boiling water and cook for 1 minute, until they float to the surface. Using a slotted spoon, transfer the gnocchi onto a lightly oiled baking sheet, preventing them from sticking to each other.

assembly Heat butter and oil in a frying pan over medium-high heat, until butter begins to froth. Add gnocchi and brown for 1 minute on each side. Transfer to a serving platter and garnish with basil and Parmesan.

grilled king oyster mushrooms and asparagus with sauce gribiche

grilled king oyster mushrooms

2 king oyster mushrooms

2 Tbsp extra-virgin olive oil

kosher salt and ground black pepper, to taste

grilled green asparagus

12 green asparagus spears, ends trimmed

2 Tbsp extra-virgin olive oil

kosher salt and ground black pepper, to taste

white asparagus

¼ c fresh lemon juice

2 Tbsp kosher salt

1 lb white asparagus, ends trimmed

3 Tbsp unsalted butter

continued facing

This is a vegetarian's dream barbecue: big, meaty king oyster mushrooms and charred asparagus with a rich French sauce dolloped overtop. King oyster mushrooms need to be cooked to bring out that savoury umami quality, while grilling creates a juicy explosion of flavour.

grilled king oyster mushrooms Preheat grill over high heat to 400°F.

Using a sharp knife, cut mushrooms in half lengthwise. Lay mushrooms flat- side down and cut lengthwise into three thin strips. Place in a bowl, season with oil, salt and pepper and gently toss.

Transfer mushrooms to a hot spot on your grill and lightly grill for 3 to 4 minutes. Turn occasionally and cook until mushrooms become slightly charred. Remove from heat and set aside.

grilled green asparagus Preheat grill over high heat to 400°F.

In a bowl, combine asparagus, oil, salt and pepper and toss.

Place onto a hot spot on your grill and grill for 2 to 3 minutes, turning occasionally, until soft, tender and nicely charred. Transfer asparagus to a cutting board. Set aside.

white asparagus In a large saucepan, combine 3 litres of water, lemon juice and salt and bring to a boil. Reduce heat to medium-low and simmer.

Carefully lay asparagus on a cutting board. Starting just below the tip, peel off the skin lengthwise using a vegetable peeler. (Careful as white asparagus is very brittle.)

Place asparagus in the water and simmer for 4 to 5 minutes, until tender or the tip of knife easily pierces the asparagus. Carefully remove asparagus from pan and drain on a paper towel.

gribiche Immerse eggs in a saucepan of water and cover. Bring to a boil over medium-high heat, then remove from heat, still covered, and set aside for 10 to 12 minutes.

Carefully drain the pan and fill with cool water to stop the cooking process. Once cool, carefully peel the shell off each egg.

Place eggs in a bowl and add Dijon, salt, pepper and a splash of olive oil. Using a fork, mash mixture until it becomes a paste. Add vinegar and the ½ cup oil and mix well. Add capers, cornichons, chervil and tarragon. Season to taste.

assembly Spoon gribiche on a serving plate. Arrange a layer of mushrooms and asparagus on top. Add more gribiche and repeat, until everything is used. Serve with watercress and radishes.

gribiche

2 large eggs

2 tsp smooth Dijon mustard

kosher salt and ground black pepper, to taste

½ c extra-virgin olive oil, plus extra for mixing

2 tsp rice vinegar

2 Tbsp capers, chopped

2 Tbsp cornichons, chopped

10 sprigs chervil, chopped

2 sprigs tarragon, chopped

assembly

shaved red radishes, to serve

watercress, to serve

lemon-sherry caramelized parsnips with charred carrot–cashew purée and crispy kale

serves 4

cashew cream

2 c raw cashews
1 tsp kosher salt

vegan butter

⅓ c ground almonds
⅓ c soy milk
2 Tbsp olive oil
1 Tbsp nutritional yeast
½ tsp kosher salt
½ tsp apple cider vinegar
¼ tsp granulated sugar
½ c canola oil

charred carrot–cashew purée

2 large carrots, skin on
3 Tbsp olive oil (divided)
kosher salt and ground black pepper, to taste
1 shallot, finely chopped
2 cloves garlic
¼ c white wine
1¼ c Vegetable Stock (p. 200)
½ c Cashew Cream (see here)
¼ c Vegan Butter (see here)
juice of ½ lemon

continued facing

This dish brings the standard parsnip and carrot medley to another level with lemon and sherry. People love this on the spot. You get the sweetness of the root veg paired with the cashew purée and crispy kale, which is essentially a vegan crouton.

cashew cream In a bowl, combine cashews and 4 cups cold water and soak for 24 hours. Drain cashews and discard the soaking water. In a blender, combine cashews, 1 cup water and salt and purée until smooth. Place in an airtight container and refrigerate until needed. (Makes 2 cups.)

vegan butter In a blender, combine ground almonds and soy milk and blend for 30 seconds, until smooth. Add olive oil, nutritional yeast, salt, vinegar and sugar and blend for another 30 seconds. With the motor still running on low, gradually pour oil into the blender. Vegan butter can be stored in an airtight container in the refrigerator for up to 2 weeks.

charred carrot–cashew purée Preheat grill over high heat to 400°F.

Using a sharp knife, carefully cut carrots lengthwise into ¼-inch-thick slices.

In a small bowl, combine carrots, 1 tablespoon oil, salt and pepper and toss. Arrange carrots on the grill and cook for 3 to 4 minutes, or until tender and lightly charred. (Be careful not to burn.)

Transfer carrots to a cutting board and roughly chop. Put them back into the bowl they were originally tossed in.

Heat the remaining 2 tablespoons oil in a frying pan over medium-low heat. Add shallots and garlic and cook for 1 minute, until fragrant. Add carrots, reduce heat to medium-low, and cook for another minute. (It's okay if they're falling apart.) Pour in wine, then bring to a boil and cook for 2 to 3 minutes, until reduced by a third.

Pour in stock and simmer for 10 minutes, until reduced by half. Stir in cashew cream and bring to a simmer. Reduce heat to low and add vegan butter. Stir in lemon juice and season to taste.

Transfer mixture to a blender and purée until smooth.

lemon-sherry caramelized parsnips Preheat oven to 400°F. Combine parsnips, maple syrup, vinegar, lemon juice, oil, salt and pepper.

Preheat an ovenproof frying pan to medium-high heat. Add parsnips, reserving liquid in bowl. Cook for 2 to 3 minutes, until parsnips begin to caramelize. Flip over and turn the pan off. Pour in the reserved liquid and add 2 tablespoons water to the pan to prevent sugars from burning.

Place pan in the preheated oven and roast parsnips for 5 minutes. Flip parsnips and roast for another 5 minutes. Roast in 5-minute intervals until parsnips are nicely caramelized and tender (about 15 minutes). (If the parsnips and sugars start to stick to the pan, add 2 more tablespoons water.)

crispy kale Heat oil in a deep fryer or deep saucepan to 350°F. (Use a thermometer for an accurate reading.) Line a baking sheet with paper towels.

Carefully lower kale into the oil and deep-fry for 30 seconds, until crispy. (Be careful not to burn.) Using a slotted spoon, transfer kale to the prepared baking sheet. Set aside.

Sriracha-maple-lime vinaigrette Measure all ingredients into a bowl and whisk until well combined. Leftover vinaigrette can be stored in the refrigerator in an airtight container for up to 2 weeks.

assembly In a small bowl, combine carrots, watercress and vinaigrette.

Spoon carrot-cashew purée onto a plate, then crisscross parsnips on top. Add fried kale leaves, then garnish with watercress-carrot mixture and drizzle with oil.

lemon-sherry caramelized parsnips

2 parsnips, peeled and cut lengthwise into long, thin wedges

1½ Tbsp maple syrup

1½ Tbsp sherry vinegar

juice of ½ lemon

3 Tbsp extra-virgin olive oil

kosher salt and ground black pepper, to taste

crispy kale

4 c canola oil

1 bunch kale, stems removed, cut into 3-inch pieces

kosher salt and ground black pepper, to taste

Sriracha-maple-lime vinaigrette

½ c fresh lime juice, strained

½ c maple syrup

2 Tbsp Sriracha

2 Tbsp rice vinegar

2 Tbsp soy sauce

1 Tbsp sesame oil

assembly

½ small carrot, thinly sliced on a mandoline

handful of watercress

2 to 3 Tbsp Sriracha-Maple-Lime Vinaigrette (see here)

extra-virgin olive oil, for drizzling

seafood

tuna tataki salad with ponzu vinaigrette

serves 4

ponzu vinaigrette
¼ c soy sauce

3 Tbsp fresh lemon juice

1½ Tbsp fresh lime juice

1½ Tbsp mirin

1 Tbsp bonito flakes

1½ tsp sake

1 (¾-inch-square) piece kombu

tuna tataki salad
1 (12-oz) piece sashimi-grade albacore tuna

1 Tbsp togarashi

kosher salt and ground black pepper, to taste

2 Tbsp vegetable oil

1 head frisée, torn into large pieces

¼ c *kaiware* (Japanese radish sprouts)

¼ red onion, thinly sliced

½ avocado, thinly sliced, for garnish

Deep-Fried Garlic Chips (p. 38), for garnish

The tuna in this dish just kisses the hot pan for a few seconds, so it's almost raw. I'm a little fanatical about my raw tuna—when I go to Hawaii, I indulge in a lot of poke. Raw or barely cooked fish is melt-in-your-mouth delicious. Make double the recipe, because you're going to want more of this fresh, clean dish.

ponzu vinaigrette In a small bowl, combine all ingredients and mix well. Set aside for up to 2 days to marinate. Strain through a fine-mesh sieve. Set aside.

tuna tataki salad Pat tuna dry with a paper towel. Season generously with togarashi, salt and pepper.

Heat oil in a frying pan over high heat, until hot but not yet smoking. Add tuna and sear each side for 10 seconds. Transfer to a plate and set aside for 1 minute. Wrap in plastic wrap and refrigerate until chilled.

Remove plastic wrap. Using a sharp knife, carefully slice the tuna into ¼-inch-thick slices.

Arrange tuna on plates and lightly garnish with frisée, kaiware and red onions. Spoon 2 tablespoons vinaigrette over each tuna salad and garnish with avocado and deep-fried garlic chips.

Sicilian tuna steak with tomato, olive and caper sauce

serves 4

If you've never barbecued fish, this is a delicious introduction to the technique. Buy high-quality tuna and keep it simple. You just want to sear the steaks: the inside should be pink and rare. That's key.

Sicilian tomato, caper and olive sauce Heat oil in a frying pan over medium heat. Add garlic, shallots, anchovies, olives and capers and sauté for 2 minutes. Pour in wine and cook for 2 minutes, until reduced by half. Add fresh and puréed tomatoes and simmer for 4 to 5 minutes. Fold in basil and parsley, then season to taste with salt and pepper. Set aside and keep warm.

tuna steaks In a medium bowl, combine oil, garlic, oregano, lemon zest and red pepper flakes and mix well. Add tuna steaks and toss gently to ensure fish is evenly coated in the mixture. Cover and refrigerate for 2 hours.

Preheat a barbecue or cast-iron grill pan over high heat to 400°F.

Wipe off excess marinade from the fish, then season with salt and pepper.

Place the tuna steaks on a hot spot on your grill and carefully grill 30 to 40 seconds. Rotate steaks 45 degrees (to get your grill marks) and cook for another 30 to 40 seconds. Turn over and repeat on the other side. Transfer tuna steaks to a plate to rest.

salad In a large bowl, combine all ingredients and toss. Adjust salt and pepper to taste.

assembly Spoon sauce into shallow bowls. Slice the tuna steaks in half and place in the centre of the sauce. Carefully arrange salad around the tuna and serve.

CHEF'S NOTE
You can substitute lemon juice for the lemon vinegar if it's not available.

Sicilian tomato, olive and caper sauce
2 Tbsp olive oil
4 cloves garlic, thinly sliced
2 shallots, sliced
2 anchovy fillets, chopped
½ c olives, pitted and quartered
¼ c capers
½ c white wine
4 Roma tomatoes, chopped
1 c canned puréed tomatoes
½ c chopped basil
½ c chopped Italian parsley
kosher salt and ground black pepper, to taste

tuna steaks
¼ c extra-virgin olive oil
4 cloves garlic, finely chopped
2 sprigs oregano, leaves only
grated zest of 1 lemon
pinch of crushed red pepper flakes
4 (3-oz) yellowfin tuna steaks
kosher salt and ground black pepper, to taste

salad
½ bunch watercress
½ head frisée, torn into large pieces
½ head radicchio, torn into large pieces
2 radishes, thinly sliced
½ c chopped basil
¼ c chopped Italian parsley
3 Tbsp + 1 tsp olive oil
4 tsp lemon vinegar
kosher salt and ground black pepper, to taste

lemon-herb grilled trout with warm lentil and spinach salad

lentils

1 c green lentils, well rinsed

4 sprigs thyme

2 cloves garlic

kosher salt and ground black pepper, to taste

warm lentil and spinach salad

4 tsp olive oil

1 c chopped walnuts

¼ c balsamic vinegar

20 asparagus tips

1 c precooked Lentils (see here)

4 c baby spinach, patted dry

kosher salt and ground black pepper

lemon-herb grilled trout

nonstick cooking spray

¼ c extra-virgin olive oil

4 cloves garlic, finely chopped

¼ c finely chopped basil

¼ c finely chopped Italian parsley

grated zest and juice of 2 lemons

4 (6-oz) skinless trout fillets

fleur de sel, to taste

ground black pepper, to taste

There's no better way to cook trout than on the barbecue. I cook it for backyard parties because it's a crowd-pleaser, and I can cook a lot of it at once. You can always substitute the trout with sea bass or red snapper.

lentils In a medium saucepan, combine all ingredients and add 4 cups cold water. Bring to a boil, then reduce heat to medium-low and simmer for 20 to 25 minutes, until lentils are tender. Drain lentils, remove thyme sprigs, then set aside to cool.

warm lentil and spinach salad Heat oil in a large frying pan over medium heat. Add walnuts and toast for 2 minutes, shaking the pan often to prevent burning. Pour in vinegar and cook for another minute, until it has a consistency that will lightly coat the walnuts. Reduce heat to low, then add asparagus tips and lentils and cook for another minute.

Turn off the heat. Add spinach and gently toss to combine. Season with salt and pepper and allow the heat of the pan to wilt the spinach. Set aside in warm pan until needed.

lemon-herb grilled trout Preheat grill over high heat to 400°F. Spray the grill with nonstick cooking spray.

In a bowl, combine oil, garlic, herbs and lemon zest and juice and mix well. Set aside.

Season trout fillets on both sides with salt and pepper, then brush both sides with the lemon-herb mixture. Grill fillets for 2 minutes, until lightly browned. Flip and grill for another 2 minutes, or until cooked through.

Transfer fillets to a plate and brush with remaining lemon-herb mixture.

assembly Mound the salad in the centre of each plate. Top with trout fillets and serve immediately.

guide to buying and cooking seafood

Fish	Texture	Taste	Fresh-Caught	Best Cooking Method	Test for Doneness
Cod	Medium	Mild	April to December	Sautéed, fried, steamed	Done when flakes easily with a fork
Halibut	Firm	Mild	March to November	Baked, sautéed, deep-fried, steamed, poached	Done when flakes easily with a fork
Rainbow trout	Medium	Moderate	Year-round	All cooking methods except steaming	Whole fish should be glistening, moist-looking at the innermost core
Ahi tuna	Firm	Moderate	Year-round	Best served rare or seared	Done when the outside of the piece of fish turns light pink and begins to flake slightly
Arctic char	Delicate	Mild	Year-round	Sautéed, broiled, baked, grilled	Done when firm to the touch and greyish in colour
Mahi mahi	Medium to firm	Moderate	Late spring/early summer	All cooking methods, especially grilling (holds its moisture well)	Done when flakes easily with a fork
Scallops	Firm	Delicate	Year-round	Best seared on high heat; also grilled, pan-fried, poached, broiled	Turns opaque when done, but centre should be barely opaque
Spot prawns	Firm	Sweet	May through June	Remove heads immediately and rinse tail or meat turns mushy. Cook ASAP. Grilled, sautéed, poached	Done after 1 or 2 minutes, when pink
Clams/mussels	Delicate	Moderate	Year-round	Steamed, baked	Done when fully open
Sockeye salmon	Firm	Full, rich	Year-round	Grilled, baked, steamed, poached, smoked	Darkish pink at centre when cooked medium
Sea bream	Medium	Lighter, sweet	Year-round	Grilled, baked, steamed, pan-fried	Done when flakes easily with a fork

pictured p. 111
serves 4

salt-crusted sea bream with almond-caper brown butter sauce

salt-crusted sea bream

6 kaffir lime leaves

2 stalks lemongrass, outer two layers discarded

2 cloves garlic

2 limes, sliced

1 c egg whites (from about 6 eggs)

2 c kosher salt

2 (1½- to 2-lb) whole sea bream, scaled and gutted

almond-caper brown butter sauce

½ c (1 stick) unsalted butter

¼ c sliced almonds

2 Tbsp capers

4 tsp fresh lemon juice

2 Tbsp chopped Italian parsley

Here's a recipe for cooks in need of a challenge. Salt-crusted fish is more common in European restaurants than in North American ones, and some cooks say this is the purest form of cooking fish. Don't worry about a salt overload—the salt crust is a cooking vessel that keeps the moisture inside the fish, and the fish's skin protects it from absorbing the salt.

salt-crusted sea bream Preheat oven to 425°F. Line a baking sheet with parchment paper.

Insert lime leaves, lemongrass, garlic and lime slices into the cavity of the fish.

In a bowl, whisk egg whites until soft peaks form. Fold in salt, until combined.

Remove pectoral fins and gills from the sea bream. Place fish onto the prepared baking sheet and pour the salt mixture overtop, patting it down to ensure that the fish is completely encased.

Bake for 25 to 30 minutes. Set aside to cool for 10 minutes.

Using the back of a knife, crack the salt crust carefully and clear salt away from the sea bream. Once it's fully exposed, carefully transfer fish to plate. With your hands, gently peel away the skin. Using a knife, slide fillets off and transfer to a serving platter. Flip fish over and repeat. Discard the salt crust.

almond-caper brown butter sauce Melt butter in a small frying pan over high heat. Add almonds and cook for 1 to 2 minutes, until they begin to brown. Remove pan from heat, then stir in capers and lightly sauté. Stir in lemon juice and parsley.

assembly Spoon the sauce over the sea bream fillets and serve immediately.

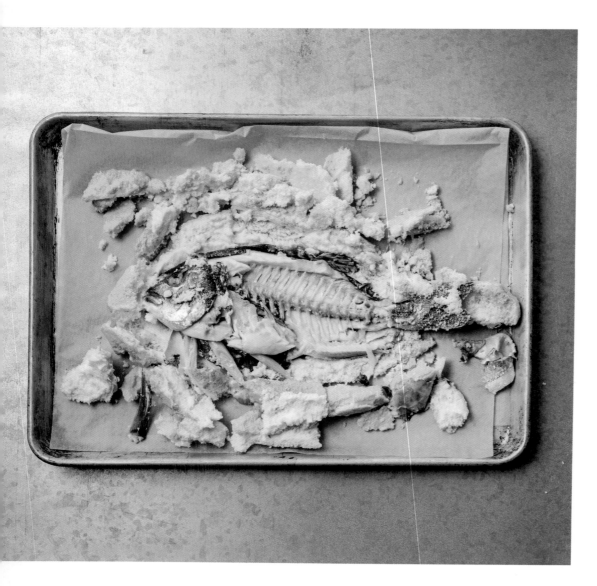

**salt-crusted
sea bream with
almond-caper
brown butter sauce**

p. 108

seafood

poached smoked sablefish
serves 4
with tarragon butter crab

The key to poaching is slow and low. You do not want your poaching liquid to boil. Give it time and you will get beautiful results. Poaching also balances out the smokiness of the sablefish, which can get a little salty.

poached smoked sablefish In a saucepan, combine milk, thyme, bay leaves and garlic and bring to a simmer over medium-low heat. Reduce heat to low, then add sablefish and poach for 6 to 8 minutes, until fish is tender. Set aside.

tarragon-butter crab Melt butter in a small saucepan over medium heat. Add leeks and sauté for 2 minutes. Add vermouth and lemon juice and cook for another minute. Pour in cream, reduce heat to medium-low and cook for another 7 to 8 minutes, until reduced by half. Stir in crabmeat and fresh herbs and simmer for 2 minutes. Season to taste with salt and pepper.

assembly Spoon the tarragon-butter crab into the centre of each plate and stack sablefish fillets on top. Serve immediately.

poached smoked sablefish

3 c milk

4 sprigs thyme

2 bay leaves

4 cloves garlic, finely chopped

4 (3-oz) smoked sablefish fillets

tarragon-butter crab

2 Tbsp unsalted butter

1 small leek, white and light green parts only, thinly sliced

6 Tbsp vermouth

juice of 1 lemon

1 c heavy (36%) cream

12 oz fresh crabmeat, picked of shells and cartilage

1 Tbsp chopped Italian parsley

1 Tbsp chopped tarragon

kosher salt and ground black pepper, to taste

fresh vs. frozen

Frozen seafood has a deservedly bad rap that's been hard to shake. But cooks need to understand that updated freezing methods mean frozen fish isn't only perfectly fine, in some cases the taste and texture is even better than fresh. I'm not promoting frozen over fresh seafood—anything that's freshly caught and delivered straight from the boat, bright-eyed and fragrant with a hint of the sea, will always be my first choice for cooking. When I worked in Bermuda, we'd serve the fish that we caught that day. But unless you're a chef with connections, it's tough to find seafood that fresh. That means it's imperative to understand the basics of blast freezing, and how a properly frozen fish compares to one that's so-called "fresh."

In a seafood production plant, there are several freezing methods, but blast freezing is the industry's finest method when it comes to the taste, texture and appearance of fish. The idea is to freeze the fish using high-velocity air circulation in order to capture the superior qualities of the raw product and preserve them. To do that, extremely cold air at a temperature of -30°F or lower is pushed across the seafood as it moves along a conveyer belt. The freezing must occur quickly so that large ice crystals don't form, which is disastrous to the cellular structure of fish—leading to a mushy product once thawed. We've all experienced a mushy piece of fish, and it's not pleasant. Blast freezing maintains the integrity of the flesh, because the ice crystals that form are small and don't break down the tissues.

In the old days, fish would be caught, filleted and kept on ice for weeks at a time, until the fishing boat returned. By then, a lot of moisture from the ice would have been absorbed into the flesh. Remember, the skin that protects the fish in the water is the skin that protects it out of the water. An intact, whole fish has retained its moisture, which is why you're always better off if you can either learn to fillet the fish yourself or ask your friendly local fishmonger to do it. It's important to have a good rapport with your local fishmonger. Find someone who is informed and has a passion for the product. Ask questions such as: When did the fish come in? Had it been previously frozen? Had it been blast frozen? How long has it been thawed? Where is it from? As well, never thaw a fish by running it under water, or letting it thaw in its own juices. Thaw fish on paper towels.

Today's freezing methods aren't the freezing methods of a couple of decades ago. So think twice when you see the "previously frozen" sign, and ask your fishmonger if it had been blast frozen. It would be a better choice than the "fresh" fish that's been sitting on ice for five days.

**halibut fish tacos
and Baja cream**

p. 116

halibut fish tacos and Baja cream

pickled red onions and jalapeños

2 jalapeños, thinly sliced into rounds

½ red onion, thinly sliced

1 c rice vinegar

2 Tbsp fresh lime juice

2 tsp kosher salt

Baja cream

½ c mayonnaise

½ c sour cream

grated zest and juice of 2 limes

kosher salt and ground black pepper, to taste

flour tortillas

2 c all-purpose flour, plus extra for dusting

1½ tsp kosher salt

1½ tsp baking powder

¼ c lard

continued facing

If you ever want to get a kid to eat fish, start with this. Kids love tacos, especially with this thick and crunchy batter. Don't be afraid to make your own tortillas. Fresh really is the best. You could swap out the battered halibut with seared tuna, barbecued trout or braised beef. Best of all, these tacos make great party food, and you can skip the cutlery.

pickled red onions and jalapeños In a bowl, combine all ingredients, then cover and place in the refrigerator to pickle for 24 hours.

Baja cream In a bowl, combine all ingredients and mix well. Season to taste. Refrigerate until needed.

flour tortillas In a medium bowl, combine flour, salt and baking powder and mix well. Using your fingers or a fork, cut lard into mixture, until it resembles a coarse cornmeal.

Stir in ½ cup water, until a soft dough forms. Add another ¼ cup water, little by little, until a ball is formed. Knead on a dry work surface for 2 to 3 minutes, until dough is soft and moist, not wet and sticky (add a little more flour if needed).

Divide dough into 1½-inch balls, then place on a baking sheet and cover with plastic wrap. Set aside to rest for 2 to 3 minutes. Dust dough balls with flour, then roll out into 3- to 4-inch disks, until nearly translucent.

Preheat a cast-iron frying pan over medium-high heat. Add a tortilla and cook for 30 to 40 seconds. Flip over and cook for another 5 seconds. (Be careful not to overcook or your tortilla will dry out.) Transfer tortilla to a plate lined with a clean dish towel and wrap in the towel until needed. Repeat with remaining tortillas. (Makes 8 to 12.)

seafood

beer batter In a medium bowl, combine flour, cornstarch, baking powder and salt. Pour in beer and whisk until smooth. Set aside for 5 minutes to rest.

halibut fish tacos Heat oil in a deep fryer or deep saucepan to 350°F. (Use a thermometer for an accurate reading.)

Pour flour into a shallow bowl. Season halibut with salt, pepper and lemon zest, then dredge in flour. Shake off any excess.

Dip halibut into beer batter, ensuring the halibut is completely coated. Carefully lower halibut into the oil and deep-fry for 2 minutes, until batter is crispy and golden brown.

Cut halibut pieces in half lengthwise and place on a platter. Serve with tortillas, Baja cream, pickled red onions and jalapeños, lettuce, cilantro and lime wedges. Enjoy!

CHEF'S NOTE
Leftover tortillas can be stored in the freezer. When ready to use, thaw and lightly toast in a frying pan over low heat.

beer batter
½ c all-purpose flour
½ c cornstarch
1 tsp baking powder
2 tsp kosher salt
1 c pale ale or lager (we prefer 33 Acres of Life beer)

halibut fish tacos
4 c oil, for deep-frying
1 c all-purpose flour, for dredging
4 oz halibut, sliced into 1-oz strips
kosher salt and ground black pepper, to taste
grated zest of 1 lemon
½ c Beer Batter (see here)
2 c thinly sliced romaine lettuce
chopped cilantro
1 lime, cut into wedges, to serve

salmon, spinach and fennel Wellington

sautéed spinach and fennel

½ Tbsp unsalted butter

½ bulb fennel, cored and cut into thin strips

1 clove garlic, finely chopped

2 c packed spinach leaves

kosher salt and ground black pepper, to taste

salmon Wellington

1 (20-oz) salmon fillet, skin removed

1 lb fresh or frozen Classic Puff Pastry (p. 202)

¾ c Sautéed Spinach and Fennel (see here)

grated zest of 1 lemon

kosher salt and ground black pepper, to taste

1 egg, beaten

salsa verde

1 clove garlic

pinch of kosher salt, plus extra to taste

1 anchovy fillet, finely chopped

1 Tbsp capers, rinsed if salted, chopped

2 Tbsp chopped Italian parsley

2 tsp strong Dijon mustard

¼ c extra-virgin olive oil

red wine vinegar, to taste

ground black pepper, to taste

This is a terrific alternative to the traditional turkey dinner: it is celebration food, dramatically presented at the table in a puff pastry crust. Inside, the salmon is flaky and moist, with anise flavour from the crunchy fennel and sweetness from the spinach. It's a meal all on its own, but great with a light side salad, too.

sautéed spinach and fennel Melt butter in a frying pan over medium heat. Add fennel and sauté for 2 to 3 minutes, until translucent and lightly browned. Add garlic and sauté for 1 minute, until fragrant. Stir in spinach and season with salt and pepper. Cook until the spinach is tender and soft.

Remove from the pan and set aside to cool. Chill until needed.

salmon Wellington Preheat oven to 425°F. Line a baking sheet with parchment paper.

Roll out the puff pastry on a cutting board until it is large enough to wrap around the salmon fillet. With a pastry brush, lightly brush egg over the top surface of the puff pastry. Spread the chilled spinach and fennel evenly along the middle of the pastry, and sprinkle with the lemon zest. Season salmon with salt and pepper and carefully place on the vegetables. Roll the pastry over the salmon, ending with the seam side down. Pinch the ends together. Brush egg on the top of the pastry.

Place the Wellington onto the prepared baking sheet and bake for 16 to 18 minutes, until golden brown on top. Set aside to rest for 10 minutes.

salsa verde Chop garlic with a pinch of salt until it turns to a paste.

In a bowl, combine garlic paste, anchovies and capers and mix well. Stir in parsley and mustard and mix together. Slowly whisk in oil.

Season with vinegar, salt and pepper to taste.

assembly Using a serrated knife, cut the salmon Wellington into four pieces and serve with salsa verde.

CHEF'S NOTE
When preparing this recipe, make sure to keep all the ingredients as cold as possible.

serves 4 # seafood motoyaki

Motoyaki is a Japanese dish that involves anything baked and topped with a mayonnaise-type sauce. We use ponzu, a citrus-based Japanese dipping sauce that pairs naturally with seafood, as the base for our aioli. As for the seafood, you can change up the type you use.

ponzu aioli In a bowl, combine yolks, garlic, 1½ tablespoons ponzu vinaigrette, mustard, togarashi, salt and sugar. Whisk in ¾ cup of the oil, until emulsified. Slowly add remaining 4½ tablespoons ponzu and half of the cheese. Add the remaining half of the oil and cheese and whisk until emulsified and it has the consistency of a loose mayonnaise.

seafood motoyaki Preheat oven to 400°F. Scrub scallop shells clean and set aside.

Heat oil in a large frying pan over medium-high heat. Add onions and mushrooms and sauté for 3 minutes, until lightly caramelized. Add spinach and fold into mixture. Set aside to cool.

Place onions, mushrooms and spinach in the bottom shell of each scallop. (Top shells can be discarded.) Randomly arrange scallops, prawns and crab on top. Spread ponzu aioli over seafood until covered. Sprinkle panko overtop, place on a baking sheet and bake for 8 minutes, until crispy and golden brown on top. Serve immediately.

ponzu aioli

2 egg yolks

2 cloves garlic, finely chopped

6 Tbsp Ponzu Vinaigrette (divided, p. 104)

2 tsp Dijon mustard

pinch of togarashi

pinch of salt

pinch of sugar

1¼ c vegetable oil

⅔ c grated Parmesan cheese

seafood motoyaki

4 fresh diver scallops, shucked and chopped, shells reserved

1 Tbsp vegetable oil

¼ c chopped onions

8 button mushrooms, thinly sliced

1 c baby spinach

4 (2½s) black tiger prawns, peeled and deveined

3 oz fresh Dungeness crabmeat, picked of shells and cartilage

panko, for sprinkling

seafood and chorizo paella

serves 4

I fell in love with paella the first time I had it in Spain. Resist the temptation to stir it. Instead, let it sit and take its time to develop the flavours and the socarrat, which is the delicious, crunchy crust that forms along the bottom of the dish. But take care not to overcook the various types of seafood. Never throw everything into the pan at once.

In a saucepan, combine stock and saffron and bring to a simmer over medium heat. Keep warm.

Heat oil in a large frying pan over medium-low heat. Add onions and sauté for 3 to 4 minutes, until translucent. Add garlic and cook for another minute. Stir in peppers, tomatoes and smoked paprika. Add rice and mix well, to ensure grains are lightly coated with oil.

Pour in stock, ensuring rice is completely submerged. Bring to a gentle simmer on medium heat and cook for 10 to 12 minutes, until rice is 75 per cent cooked. Be careful not to boil or let the pan go dry; add more stock if needed.

Add mussels, clams, prawns, squid and chorizo to the pan and cover. Lower heat to medium-low and cook for another 5 minutes, until rice absorbs remaining stock and is completely cooked, and mussels and clams have opened. (Do not stir in seafood.) Fold in peas and cover. Set aside to rest for 5 minutes.

To finish, add parsley and season to taste with salt, pepper and lemon juice.

4 c Chicken Stock (p. 200), plus extra if needed

30 threads saffron

2 Tbsp extra-virgin olive oil

½ onion, chopped

4 cloves garlic, finely chopped

10 piquillo peppers, seeded, deveined and chopped

2 Roma tomatoes, chopped

1 tsp smoked paprika

1½ c bomba rice

15 mussels, scrubbed clean

15 clams, scrubbed clean

12 prawns, peeled and deveined

12 squid, cleaned and halved

6 oz Spanish chorizo, cut into a ½-inch dice

1 c fresh or frozen peas (see Note)

¼ c chopped Italian parsley kosher salt and ground black pepper, to taste

juice of ½ lemon, or to taste

CHEF'S NOTE
When using fresh peas, add with seafood instead to allow a longer cooking time.

poultry
and
meats

roasted chicken breast with
West Coast panzanella salad

serves 4 (small plates)

This peasant-style dish has a great flavour profile and a lot of textures. The roasted chicken, crisp bread and sharp vinaigrette together make a delicious combo. To get that crispy skin, cook the chicken skin-side down, and resist any temptation to turn it over.

roasted chicken breast Preheat oven to 400°F.

Season chicken with salt and pepper.

Heat oil in an ovenproof frying pan over medium heat. Add chicken, skin-side down, and sear for 20 to 30 seconds. Place pan in oven and roast for 10 to 12 minutes, or until the internal temperature reaches 165°F on a meat thermometer.

West Coast panzanella salad Preheat oven to 400°F.

In a small bowl, combine torn sourdough, 3 tablespoons oil, half the garlic, salt and pepper, and toss to mix. Transfer to a baking sheet and toast in the oven for 5 to 6 minutes, until lightly crispy. Set aside.

In a separate bowl, combine capers, vinegar, remaining half of the garlic, remaining ⅓ cup oil, parsley and lemon zest and juice and mix well.

In another bowl, combine tomatoes, cucumber, bell peppers, fennel, olives, basil, fennel fronds, if using, and cheese. Pour in vinaigrette and toasted sourdough and lightly toss together. Season to taste with salt, pepper and lemon juice.

assembly Divide salad among 4 plates. Slice chicken into ¼-inch-thick slices and place them next to the salad.

roasted chicken breast

2 skin-on, boneless chicken breasts

kosher salt and ground black pepper

1 Tbsp vegetable oil

West Coast panzanella salad

1¼ c torn rustic sourdough

⅓ c + 3 Tbsp extra-virgin olive oil (divided)

2 cloves garlic, finely chopped (divided)

kosher salt and ground black pepper, to taste

2 Tbsp capers, chopped

4 tsp red wine vinegar

2 Tbsp chopped Italian parsley

grated zest and juice of 1 lemon, plus extra to taste

2 tomatoes, cut into small pieces

⅓ c peeled and diced seedless cucumber

¼ red bell pepper, seeded, deveined and cut into thin strips

¼ bulb fennel, thinly shaved

12 niçoise olives

8 basil leaves, torn

¼ c fennel fronds (optional)

1 Tbsp grated Parmesan cheese

Thai chicken curry

Thai chicken curry

8 skinless, boneless chicken thighs, halved

kosher salt and ground black pepper

2 Tbsp vegetable oil

¼ c Green Curry Paste (p. 199)

3 c coconut milk

2 Tbsp light brown sugar

2 tsp fish sauce

2 kaffir lime leaves, torn

1 c chopped long beans or green beans, cut into 2-inch segments

½ c firmly packed Thai basil leaves (divided)

stir-fried corn and cashews

2 cobs corn

1 Tbsp vegetable oil

½ red onion, sliced

½ red bell pepper, seeded, deveined and cut into thin strips

¼ c cashew nuts

1 green onion, chopped

1 Tbsp soy sauce

assembly

steamed rice, to serve

If there's one cuisine I could eat for rest of my life it would be Thai food, and I've been blessed because my Thai sister-in-law, Tula, is a terrific cook. You can make the green curry paste with a mortar and pestle or a modern-day food processor. Make it in advance and keep it in the freezer—and voilà, you have an instantly complex meal in no time at all.

Thai chicken curry Season chicken with salt and pepper.

Heat oil in a saucepan over medium heat. Add curry paste and chicken and sauté for a minute. Pour in coconut milk, then add sugar, fish sauce and kaffir lime leaves and bring to a boil. Reduce heat to a simmer and cook for 15 to 20 minutes, until sauce starts to coat the chicken. Add beans and half the basil and cook, stirring occasionally, for 2 to 3 minutes, until the beans are tender and the chicken is cooked through. Cover and keep warm on low heat.

stir-fried corn and cashews Bring a large saucepan of salted water to a boil. Add corn and boil for 5 to 7 minutes. Cut kernels off the cobs.

Heat oil in a frying pan over medium heat. Add corn, onions, bell peppers and cashews and sauté for 2 minutes. Reduce heat to medium-low, stir in soy sauce and add green onion. Cook for another 30 seconds.

assembly Serve curry in individual bowls or a large serving bowl. Top with corn and cashews and remaining basil leaves. Serve with rice.

pictured p.132
makes 3 small pizzas

burrata and prosciutto pizza

burrata

2 Tbsp kosher salt

1 lb mozzarella curds, cut into ¼-inch pieces

3 Tbsp heavy (36%) cream

2 Tbsp ricotta

1 tsp unsalted butter, melted

pizza sauce

2 Tbsp extra-virgin olive oil

¼ c finely chopped onions

3 cloves garlic, finely chopped

2 c puréed tomatoes

2 Tbsp chopped thyme

kosher salt and ground black pepper, to taste

burrata and prosciutto pizza

1 quantity Pizza Dough (p. 201)

all-purpose flour, for dusting

1½ c Pizza Sauce (see here)

2 Burrata (see here), cut into ½-inch cubes

6 slices prosciutto, cut into 2-inch pieces

bunch of basil, torn extra-virgin olive oil, for drizzling

A lot of our customers have requested a recipe for a good pizza, so here we go. And when I say it's from scratch, I'm not just talking about the dough. Don't be intimidated by making your own burrata cheese. It requires a little technique, but you can't go too wrong by starting with good-quality, store-bought mozzarella curds.

burrata Combine 4 cups water and the salt in a medium saucepan over medium heat and bring to a simmer. Place curds in a medium bowl and pour in the hot salted water. Soak curds for 2 to 3 minutes.

Meanwhile, fill a small bowl halfway with ice cubes, then add enough cold water to fill to three-quarters.

With gloved hands, carefully gather the cheese curds. which should feel soft. Keeping your hands submerged, knead curds for 1 to 2 minutes until smooth, soft and pliable. (If your hands get too hot while kneading, briefly dip them into the bowl of cold water and continue.) Be careful not to over-work the curds—the more you knead, the firmer they become. Form curds into a ball and transfer to a cutting board, reserving the saltwater solution.

Using a knife, cut off a third of the ball and place into the ice bath. Cut the remaining ball in half and form each half into a ball. With your hands, care-fully flatten and stretch into 6-inch disks. Set aside.

In a small bowl, combine cream, ricotta and melted butter. With a spoon, skim the whey gathered on the surface of the saltwater solution. Add 3 table-spoons of it to the ricotta mixture. Retrieve burrata curd from ice bath and shred into small pieces with your hands. Add these pieces to the ricotta mixture and mix until creamy. If the mixture seems dry, add more saltwater solution.

Line a small bowl (about the size of a 2-oz ladle) with one flattened bur-rata disk, taking care not to tear the burrata. Spoon half of the burrata filling into the centre of the cupped burrata disk. Carefully gather the sides of the burrata into one hand and gently twist.

While you hold the burrata, ask a friend to tie a piece of the butcher's twine around the neck of the twisted burrata. Do your best to ensure there are no holes or leaks.

Place burrata into an ice bath to cool and retain its shape. Repeat with remaining burrata disk and filling. Burrata can be refrigerated for up to 4 to 5 days.

pizza sauce Heat oil in a small saucepan over medium heat. Add onions and sauté for 7 minutes, until onions become soft and translucent. Add garlic and sauté for another minute, until fragrant.

Add tomatoes and thyme and bring to a boil, then reduce heat to medium-low and simmer for about 40 minutes. Season to taste with salt and pepper. Set aside to cool.

burrata and prosciutto pizza Place a large baking sheet upside down on the lowest shelf in the oven and preheat to 550°F.

Cut proofed pizza dough in thirds and roll into three smaller balls. Place dough onto a floured surface and use a rolling pin to roll it out as thinly as possible. Take a fork and lightly dock the dough 10 to 15 times around the dough's surface.

With a spoon, spread the sauce over the pizza shells.

Transfer pizza shells to a large piece of aluminum foil and carefully place them, along with the foil, onto the preheated baking sheet. Bake for 2 to 3 minutes, or until the crust is crispy. Arrange burrata and prosciutto on top and cook for another minute. Remove from the oven, add basil and finish with a drizzle of olive oil. Enjoy!

CHEF'S NOTE
Special equipment: 1 pair of food-grade gloves and 2 (12-inch) pieces of butcher's twine.

burrata and
prosciutto pizza
p. 130

how to make the perfect pizza

Making your own pizza with friends and family is an enjoyable cooking experience. No matter how misshapen, sloppy or charred, homemade pizza is infinitely better than your average delivery options.

1 Base	**2** Sauce	**3** Toppings	**4** Garnish
Flatbread (p. 160)	Baba Ganoush (p. 148)	Burrata (p. 130)	Arugula
Gluten-Free Naan Bread (p. 170)	Hummus (p. 90)	Confit Tomatoes (p. 93)	Crispy Kale (p. 101)
Herb and Garlic Confit Focaccia (p. 163)	Pesto (p. 198)	Gravlax (p. 25)	Fresh herbs
Pizza Dough (p. 201)	Pizza Sauce (p. 131)	Grilled meat or fish	Nuts
	Salsa Verde (p. 145)	Roasted garlic	Olive oil
	Tomato Salsa	Spanish chorizo	Shaved Parmesan cheese
			Watercress

Place a large baking sheet upside down on the lowest shelf in the oven and preheat to 550°F. With a spoon, spread your preferred sauce over the base. Place base on a large piece of aluminum foil and carefully place it, along with the foil, onto the preheated baking sheet. Bake for 2 to 3 minutes, or until cooked through. Arrange your favourite toppings on top and cook for another minute. Remove from the oven, add your garnishes and serve.

sake-braised pork belly with sesame rice cakes

serves 4 to 6

sake-braised pork belly

2 lbs skin-on pork belly, cut into 8 pieces

sea salt and ground black pepper

2 Tbsp vegetable oil

½ large onion, chopped

knob of ginger, coarsely chopped

4 cloves garlic, sliced

1 small leek, white and light green parts only, cut into ½-inch slices

6 Tbsp granulated sugar

⅔ c soy sauce

⅓ c sake

2 star anise

1 Tbsp sesame seeds, for garnish

2 Tbsp sliced green onions, for garnish

sesame rice cakes

2 c Japanese short-grain rice

¼ c sesame seeds, toasted

vegetable oil, for frying

The crispy rice cakes pair well with the rich, succulent pork belly. The next day, pull the pork apart and load it up on a toasted baguette for a fantastic sandwich. We braise the pork belly a day or two ahead so all the juices soak into the meat.

sake-braised pork belly Preheat oven to 350°F.

Pat pork belly dry with paper towels, then season generously with salt and pepper.

Heat oil in a large ovenproof frying pan over medium-high heat. Add pork belly and sear for 4 minutes, until golden brown on all sides. Transfer pork belly to a plate and set aside.

In the same pan, sauté onions, ginger, garlic and leeks over medium heat for 3 to 4 minutes, until softened. Transfer mixture to a plate and set aside.

In the same pan, combine sugar and 1 tablespoon of water and cook over high heat until sugar is caramelized and golden brown. Add pork belly to the pan and use tongs to carefully roll it around in the mixture.

Pour in soy sauce and sake, then add star anise, sautéed vegetables and enough water to fully submerge the pork belly. Bring to a boil and cover. Braise in the oven for 90 minutes, or until pork is tender. Using tongs, transfer pork to a plate. Strain braising liquid, discarding solids, and cook for 10 to 15 minutes, until syrupy. Return pork to the pan and stir. Set aside and keep warm.

sesame rice cakes Place rice in a bowl and rinse with cold water. Drain and repeat until water runs clear. Drain rice.

Combine rice and 2½ cups water in a rice cooker and cook. (Alternatively, combine rice and water in a saucepan and cover with a lid. Bring to a boil, then reduce heat to low and simmer for 12 minutes. Do not remove the lid! Turn off heat and set pan aside, covered, for another 10 minutes.)

Transfer rice to a bowl and carefully break rice apart with a wet wooden spoon. Stir in sesame seeds.

Fill a large bowl with cold water. (Dipping your hands in the water will make the rice easier to handle.) On a cutting board, fill a 2- or 3-inch ring cutter with rice and pat to a ½-inch thickness. Set rice cake aside and repeat with remaining rice.

Heat oil in a frying pan over high heat. Add rice cakes and cook for 2 to 3 minutes on each side, until golden brown and edges crisp.

assembly Place rice cakes on a serving dish and ladle pork and sauce on top. Garnish with sesame seeds and green onions.

South Indian–spiced pork tenderloin with lemon rice

serves 4

South Indian rub

3 Tbsp fleur de sel

2 Tbsp brown sugar

1 Tbsp ground cinnamon

2 Tbsp cumin seeds

1 Tbsp coriander seeds

2 tsp green cardamom

1 Tbsp ground turmeric

2 tsp garam masala

lemon rice

2⅔ c cooked basmati rice

2 Tbsp vegetable oil (divided)

grated zest and juice of 1 lemon

kosher salt and ground black pepper, to taste

2 Tbsp chopped cashews

2 tsp black mustard seeds

20 fresh curry leaves (or 10 dried curry leaves)

4 tsp grated ginger

4 tsp crushed red pepper flakes

½ tsp ground turmeric

pork tenderloin

2 Tbsp vegetable oil

1 (1-lb) pork tenderloin, patted dry, divided into 4 pieces

6 Tbsp South Indian-Spiced Rub (see here)

assembly

cilantro, for garnish

Pork tenderloins are a midweek favourite, and here they're elevated with a blend of Indian spices and topped off with grilled smokiness. Don't be afraid to cook pork medium-rare for maximum juiciness. This tenderloin dish is so flavourful, you won't need a sauce.

South Indian rub In a small bowl, combine fleur de sel, brown sugar and cinnamon.

In a mortar and pestle, coarsely grind cumin seeds, coriander seeds and cardamom. Place in a dry frying pan and toast over medium-high heat for 1 minute, until toasted and fragrant. Turn off heat, then add turmeric and garam masala to pan and toss lightly. Set aside to cool.

Add toasted spices to the brown sugar-cinnamon mixture and toss until well combined. Transfer to airtight container and store for up to 3 months.

lemon rice In a medium bowl, combine rice, 1 tablespoon oil, lemon zest and juice, salt and pepper and toss well. Set aside.

Heat remaining 1 tablespoon oil in a frying pan over medium-low heat. Add cashews and toast lightly. Add mustard seeds and stir constantly, until the mustard seeds start to pop. Quickly add curry leaves, ginger and red pepper flakes and cook for 2 minutes, until curry leaves are crisp. Turn off heat. Add turmeric and stir for another minute to prevent the mixture from burning.

Transfer ingredients to the bowl with rice. Gently mix together and season to taste with salt and pepper. Serve hot or cold.

pork tenderloin Preheat oven to 350°F.

Heat oil in a large ovenproof frying pan over medium-high heat. Season pork tenderloin with salt and pepper, then generously rub with the spice rub, ensuring tenderloin is coated evenly.

Add tenderloin to the pan and sear for 30 seconds on each side, until browned. Place pan into oven and cook for 5 minutes. Flip over and roast for 7 to 8 minutes, or until the internal temperature reaches 140°F on a meat thermometer. Set aside to rest for 3 to 4 minutes before slicing.

assembly Thinly slice pork and arrange over rice on individual plates. Garnish with cilantro and serve immediately.

coconut-lemongrass braised beef short ribs

serves 4

In our first cookbook, we included our popular short ribs recipe. We take the same cut of beef short rib to another level here with a journey through Thailand. The protein breaks down in a creamy coconut braise infused with aromatics. The aroma of this dish will keep your family hanging around the kitchen.

Preheat oven to 350°F.

Heat oil in a large frying pan over high heat. Generously season beef with salt and pepper. Add beef to pan and sear for a minute. Turn and sear for another minute. Repeat until all four sides are seared. Turn off the heat. Transfer beef to a heavy-bottomed ovenproof saucepan or Dutch oven.

In the same frying pan, cook shallots, lemongrass and ginger for 2 to 3 minutes on low heat. Add garlic and curry paste, turn heat back to high and sauté for 30 seconds. Stir in coconut cream and fish sauce, until coconut cream is fully incorporated. Add kaffir lime leaves, palm (or brown) sugar, lime juice and oyster sauce and stir until sugar is completely dissolved. Bring mixture to a boil and turn off heat.

Pour mixture over beef. Cover pan with lid or aluminum foil and cook for 2 to 2½ hours, until fork tender. Serve with rice.

1 Tbsp vegetable oil

2 lbs boneless beef short ribs, cut into 4-oz pieces (8 in total)

sea salt and ground black pepper

3 shallots, chopped

2 stalks lemongrass, outer two layers discarded

3 Tbsp chopped ginger

6 cloves garlic, chopped

3 Tbsp Red Curry Paste (p. 199)

4 cups full-fat coconut cream (see Note)

3 Tbsp fish sauce

10 kaffir lime leaves

¼ c palm or brown sugar

2 Tbsp fresh lime juice

2 Tbsp oyster sauce

steamed rice, to serve

CHEF'S NOTE
Coconut cream contains much less water than coconut milk, which results in a smoother, thicker and richer consistency.

killer rib-eye steak and truffle pomme purée

serves 4

truffle pomme purée

2 large golden Yukon Gold potatoes, unpeeled

kosher salt and ground white pepper, to taste

½ c heavy (36%) cream

¼ c (½ stick) unsalted butter, room temperature

truffle oil, to taste

red wine sauce

1 Tbsp extra-virgin olive oil

1 shallot, finely chopped

1 clove garlic, finely chopped

⅓ c dry red wine

⅓ c Beef Stock (p. 201)

2 Tbsp unsalted butter, cold

kosher salt and ground black pepper, to taste

rib-eye steaks

2 Tbsp olive oil

4 Tbsp maple syrup

4 Tbsp soy sauce

4 Tbsp sherry vinegar

4 cloves garlic, finely chopped

4 sprigs thyme

4 sprigs rosemary

kosher salt and ground black pepper, to taste

4 (4- to 8-oz) rib-eye steaks

fleur de sel, to season

A great steak recipe is essential in every good cook's repertoire—it's the go-to for when you want to impress. The marinade is what makes this recipe sing. You've got the sweet maple syrup, the salty soy and sharp sherry vinegar, the punch of garlic—once the grilling has seared the meat, it adds up to the perfect bite.

truffle pomme purée Put potatoes in a saucepan and add enough water to cover them by 2 inches. Add ½ tablespoon of salt and bring to a boil. Simmer gently for 30 minutes, or until potatoes are tender. Drain.

While the potatoes are still warm, peel off skins. Press potatoes through a food mill into a bowl to obtain a smooth, lump-free texture. (Alternatively, use a masher.)

In a medium saucepan, heat cream over medium heat until it nearly comes to a boil. Add butter and potato and use a rubber spatula to slowly fold them in, until it becomes a smooth purée. Add truffle oil, salt and pepper to taste. (A little goes a long way. Add a few drops at a time until the desired flavour is reached.) Keep warm until needed.

red wine sauce Heat oil in a small saucepan over medium heat. Add shallots and garlic and sauté for 2 minutes, until soft but not browned. Pour in wine and stock, increase heat to medium-high and cook for another 2 to 3 minutes, until mixture is reduced by a third. Whisk in butter, a little at a time, then season with salt and pepper.

Strain sauce through a fine-mesh sieve, and discard solids. Keep warm.

rib-eye steaks In a medium bowl, combine all ingredients, except the steaks, and mix well. Add steaks and mix to coat, then cover and refrigerate for 2 hours to marinate.

Preheat grill over high heat to 400°F.

Remove steaks from the marinade and pat dry with a paper towel, then season with fleur de sel. Grill for 4 to 5 minutes, then flip and grill for another 4 to 5 minutes, for medium-rare, or until the internal temperature reaches 125°F on a meat thermometer.

Transfer steaks to a plate and set aside to rest for 5 minutes. Serve steaks with truffle pomme purée and top with red wine sauce.

Korean barbecue short ribs

serves 4 to 6

5 lbs beef short ribs, ¼-inch cross-cut on the bone (ask your butcher)

1 c packed brown sugar

1 small onion, chopped

1 small Asian pear, peeled and chopped into ½-inch cubes

1 c soy sauce

¼ c mirin

¼ c finely chopped garlic

2 Tbsp dark sesame oil

¼ tsp ground black pepper

2 green onions, thinly sliced, for garnish (optional)

When I worked in Switzerland, it so happened that we had a lot of Korean cooks in the kitchen. They inspired me to create this recipe based on the classic Korean barbecue short ribs known as *kalbi*, but with the sweetness of pear infusing the marinade. Feel free to change it up with pineapple, kiwi or any other high-sugar fruit. This marinade works equally well on chicken thighs.

Sprinkle short ribs with brown sugar and mix well to evenly coat. Set aside at room temperature for 10 minutes.

Meanwhile, prepare the marinade. In a food processor or blender, combine the remaining ingredients (except the green onions), add ½ cup water and blend until smooth.

Transfer short ribs into a large freezer bag (you may need two). Pour in marinade, press out excess air and seal. Turn bag(s) over several times to ensure short ribs are evenly coated. Refrigerate for at least 4 hours but preferably overnight.

Preheat grill over high heat to 400°F. Drain excess marinade off short ribs, then add them to the grill. Grill for 3 to 4 minutes per side, turning once only.

Transfer short ribs to a serving plate and garnish with green onions (if using).

barbecue basics

As the son of a Scottish butcher, let's just say that I know my way around a cut of meat. During the summer, I'm at the barbecue pretty much every day, whether it's grilling steak, fish or veggies. Nothing speaks of summer like a platter of grilled meats or seafood, a big salad and family and friends dining outdoors.

I prefer a wood-burning barbecue, but you can use propane or charcoal. It's a matter of preference. Whatever you use, be sure to pay attention to a few key rules of barbecuing, to ensure that you don't end up with a piece of chicken that's black on the outside and pink on the inside, or a steak that's burst into flames.

To start, find a great marinade. You don't have to marinate your beef, but it infuses the meat with such fantastic flavour, I don't see why you wouldn't. I love marinades that marry sweet, like maple syrup, with the acidity of soy, citrus or a good-quality vinegar. The Killer Rib-Eye Steak and Truffle Pomme Purée (p. 140) is a great example of this happy union. And when you grill it, the sugars sear into the meat, the fat caramelizes and gets crispy, and the saltiness ramps up those flavours—the whole thing just sings. When cooking chicken, brine it overnight to make it especially juicy. You can then baste it in a sauce as it finishes cooking. However you don't want to baste it with a sugary sauce at a high heat for a long time, because sugar burns.

Start with a clean grill that's been scraped of any residue and is oiled up and ready to go. You don't want to be cooking three-day-old bitter bits of charred meat.

Next is the temperature. Bring your steak to room temperature so that you can better control the timing. And before your meat goes anywhere near the grill, be sure that your barbecue is hot and ready. You want to create a heated area inside the barbecue between 375°F and 400°F. You also want another area that is at a lower temperature of about 200°F, to keep food warm without overcooking. On my barbecue, I move meats from the hottest point in the middle to the left, where it's cooler.

You should also know your product, and whether it gets cooked low and slow or hot and fast. A lot of cuts of meat, such as a rib-eye steak—a barbecue cook's best friend—benefit from a quick sear on the hottest part of the grill, before moving over to finish cooking on the cooler part of the grill. Don't overcook by keeping it over the high heat.

Be sure to learn how to test for doneness, either by using a meat thermometer or by touching the meat. An internal temperature of around 120°F is rare; 125°F medium-rare; 130°F is medium; and 135°F is medium-well. If you don't have a thermometer, a tried-and-true test is that a rare piece of meat, when poked, feels like the fatty part of your hand, at the base of your thumb. If you hold your first finger and thumb together and poke the fleshy part of your hand, that's how a medium-rare steak should feel. If you let it cook firmer than that, you're going to get a medium-cooked steak.

And finally, be sure to rest your meat for at least five minutes to retain moisture. If you don't rest your steak or chicken, the juices will pour out when you cut into it. And there goes the moisture.

Follow these tips, and you too might find yourself spending your summer evenings with tongs in hand, happily sipping a beer as you preside over the barbecue.

beef tenderloin, salsa verde, honey-roasted carrots and yams

serves 2

honey-roasted yams

2 medium yams, unpeeled

½ c honey

¼ c extra-virgin olive oil

kosher salt and ground black pepper

honey-roasted carrots

3 Tbsp sherry vinegar

3 Tbsp honey

¼ c olive oil

8 baby carrots

pinch of salt

pinch of ground black pepper

continued facing

This show-stopping dish makes an impression on guests. Medallions of beef tenderloin are served alongside yams and carrots that have been roasted and intensified with honey and vinegar. The yams are prepared hasselback-style, which means they're thinly sliced about halfway through, keeping the yams intact. The salsa verde adds just the right hint of acidity to balance out these comforting, grounded flavours.

honey-roasted yams Preheat oven to 400°F.

To make the hasselback yams, place one yam on a board between the handles of two wooden spoons. (This way, when you slice down into the yam, the spoons prevent the blade from going all the way through.) Carefully slice at ¼-inch intervals all the way along. Repeat with the remaining yam.

In a bowl, combine honey, oil, salt and pepper. Add yams and toss to coat.

Place yams in a baking dish, add ½ cup water and roast, uncovered, for 30 minutes, or until soft and tender. Keep warm until needed.

honey-roasted carrots Preheat oven to 400°F.

In a bowl, combine vinegar, honey and oil. Add carrots and toss to generously coat. Season with salt and pepper.

Arrange carrots in a single layer in a roasting pan. Bake for 15 to 20 minutes, until carrots are cooked through and have a bit of colour. (Watch them carefully so you don't burn or overcook them.) Set aside to cool.

salsa verde Chop garlic with a little pinch of salt until it has a paste-like consistency.

In a bowl, combine anchovies, garlic and capers. Stir in parsley, mint and mustard. Slowly add oil, whisking continuously. Season with vinegar, salt and pepper to taste. Salsa verde can be refrigerated in an airtight container for up to 2 days.

beef tenderloin Preheat oven to 400°F. Season beef with salt and pepper.

Heat oil in a large ovenproof frying pan over high heat. Add medallions and sear for 30 seconds on each side. Put pan into the oven and roast for 4 to 5 minutes, or until the internal temperature reaches 125°F on a meat thermometer for medium-rare. Transfer medallions to a plate and set aside to rest for 5 minutes.

Add Brussels sprouts leaves to the pan and sauté for 1 minute, until slightly wilted. Season to taste with salt and pepper.

assembly Divide carrots and yams between two serving plates. Add 2 medallions to each plate, then top with Brussels sprout leaves and salsa verde. Serve immediately.

salsa verde

1 small clove garlic

pinch of kosher salt, plus extra to taste

1 anchovy fillet, finely chopped

1 Tbsp capers, rinsed and roughly chopped

½ c Italian parsley leaves, roughly chopped

1 Tbsp mint leaves, roughly chopped

1 Tbsp Dijon mustard

⅓ c extra-virgin olive oil

red wine vinegar, to taste

ground black pepper, to taste

beef tenderloin

4 (3-oz) beef tenderloin medallions

sea salt and ground black pepper

1 Tbsp vegetable oil

2 c Brussels sprouts leaves

Spanish manchego meatballs with saffron basmati rice

serves 5

saffron basmati rice

1 tsp kosher salt

1 c basmati rice

2 Tbsp olive oil

4 to 6 cloves garlic, thinly sliced

1 onion, chopped

pinch of saffron

1 Tbsp chopped Italian parsley

roasted red pepper–tomato sauce

2 large red bell peppers

½ c olive oil

1 large onion, chopped

½ c finely chopped garlic

5 cups whole tomatoes

1 tsp crushed red pepper flakes

2 Tbsp chopped Italian parsley

kosher salt and ground black pepper, to taste

continued facing

What separates these meatballs from your run-of-the-mill meatballs is that we soak the brioche pieces so they stay extremely moist when they come out of the oven. It's an Italian meatball trick I learned early on, while working with an Italian chef.

saffron basmati rice   Bring 2 litres of water and salt to a boil in a large saucepan. Add rice, cover and boil for 12 minutes. Turn off heat and let the rice sit for another 10 minutes. Drain rice.

Heat oil in a frying pan over medium-high heat. Add garlic and sauté for 2 minutes, until golden brown. Transfer to a bowl and set aside for garnish.

In the same pan, mix together rice, onions and saffron and sauté for 3 minutes. Transfer to a serving dish. Garnish with parsley and reserved garlic. Cover to keep warm until serving.

roasted red pepper–tomato sauce   Preheat oven to 450°F. Line a baking sheet with aluminum foil.

Place peppers on the prepared baking sheet and roast for 35 minutes, or until peppers are charred. Remove peppers from the oven and set aside until cool enough to handle.

Remove the outer skins, stems and seeds and halve lengthwise.

Heat oil in a deep saucepan over medium heat. Add onions and garlic and sauté for 2 to 3 minutes, until the garlic is golden brown. Add peppers and tomatoes and simmer over medium-low heat for 30 minutes.

Turn off heat. Using an immersion blender, purée mixture until smooth. Stir in red pepper flakes and parsley. Season to taste with salt and pepper. Keep warm over low heat until use.

manchego meatballs Preheat oven to 425°F. Line a baking sheet with parchment paper.

In a small bowl, combine brioche pieces and 1 cup cold water and soak for 5 minutes.

In a large bowl, combine beef, pork, eggs, Parmesan, parsley, smoked paprika, salt, pepper and soaked brioche and use your hands to mix well. In a small frying pan over medium-high heat, fry a small amount of the mixture until cooked through. Taste it and adjust seasoning if needed.

Portion out ½-cup measures of meat mixture and form balls. (Makes about 10.) Place meatballs onto the prepared baking sheet and bake for 8 minutes. Flip and bake for another 10 minutes.

Place a small slice of manchego cheese on top of each meatball and bake for 1 to 2 minutes, until cheese has melted.

assembly Pour red pepper–tomato sauce into a casserole dish and arrange meatballs on top. Garnish with parsley and a drizzle of olive oil. Serve with saffron basmati rice!

manchego meatballs

2 c brioche pieces, white part only, cut into 1-inch cubes

2 lbs ground beef

½ lb ground pork

2 large eggs

¼ c grated Parmesan cheese

1 Tbsp chopped Italian parsley

1 Tbsp smoked paprika

2 tsp kosher salt

1 tsp ground black pepper

2 oz manchego cheese, thinly sliced

assembly

1 Tbsp chopped Italian parsley

extra-virgin olive oil, for drizzling

roasted lamb with baba ganoush, tahini vinaigrette and flatbread

serves 4

baba ganoush
2 large eggplants
6 cloves garlic
¾ c plain yogurt
2 tsp cumin seeds, toasted and ground
juice of 2 lemons
1 c extra-virgin olive oil
kosher salt and ground black pepper, to taste

tahini vinaigrette
½ c olive oil
¼ c tahini
2 cloves garlic, finely chopped
grated zest and juice of 1 lemon
kosher salt and ground black pepper, to taste

roasted lamb loins
2 cloves garlic, finely chopped
¼ c olive oil
grated zest of 1 lemon
2 tsp sumac
2 tsp ground cumin
2 tsp coriander seeds, coarsely ground
4 (4-oz) lamb loins
sea salt and ground black pepper, to season

assembly
4 Flatbreads (p. 160)
1 c arugula

This dish looks impressive on a plate. It's a dish that's easy to pull off, and yet the levels of flavour are complex, with the tangy yogurt, toasty cumin seeds and slightly bitter tahini.

baba ganoush Preheat oven to 450°F.

Place eggplants on a baking sheet and roast for 40 minutes, until they are soft and have collapsed in on themselves. Remove from the oven and carefully cut a slit down the centre of each to allow the steam to escape.

Scrape out the pulp into a food processor or blender, then add garlic, yogurt, cumin and lemon juice. Blend until smooth. With the motor still running, slowly incorporate oil until emulsified. Season with salt and pepper. Set aside.

tahini vinaigrette In a bowl, combine oil, tahini and garlic and mix well. Add lemon zest and juice, and season with salt and pepper to taste. Set aside.

roasted lamb loins Preheat oven to 400°F.

In a bowl, combine garlic, oil, lemon zest and spices and mix well. Add lamb and coat well. Set aside in the refrigerator for 1 hour to marinate.

Heat an ovenproof frying pan over high heat. Season lamb with salt and pepper, then add to the pan and sear for 30 seconds on each side, until browned. Place pan into the oven and roast for 4 to 5 minutes, for rare to medium-rare doneness. Set lamb aside for 5 minutes to rest.

assembly Place flatbreads on individual plates and spread with baba ganoush. Thinly slice the lamb loins and arrange on top. In a small bowl, combine the arugula and with 2 tablespoons tahini vinaigrette and place it on top of the lamb.

CHEF'S NOTE
To barbecue, preheat a grill over high heat to 400°F. Add lamb to grill and rotate every 2 minutes, until desired doneness. (About 8 to 10 minutes for medium-rare, or once the internal temperature reaches 125°F.)

serves 4   **Auntie Zakia's lamb curry**

When our employees start at the Dirty Apron, we ask them to make their favourite dish for the staff meal. Auntie Zakia, as she's lovingly called by our staff, made us her lamb curry. It was such a hit that we put it on our menu. Customers flipped out, so naturally we had to include it here.

Preheat oven to 350°F.

    Season lamb with salt and pepper. Heat 1 tablespoon oil in a Dutch oven over high heat. Add lamb and sear for a minute. Turn and sear for another minute. Transfer lamb to a bowl.

    Heat 1 teaspoon oil in the same pan. Combine onions, ginger, cinnamon stick, cardamom and bay leaves and sauté over medium-low heat for a minute. Add the remaining tablespoon of oil and sauté for 2 minutes. Add garlic and sauté for another 30 seconds. Add coriander, cumin, curry powder, turmeric, cayenne, fennel seeds and garam masala. Sauté for 4 to 5 minutes, until all ingredients are evenly coated in the spices.

    Add puréed tomatoes, bell peppers, squeeze of lemon juice, lemon wedge and ⅓ cup water and simmer for 30 seconds. Add lamb and mix well. Add vinegar and bring to a boil, then remove from heat and season to taste with salt and pepper. Cover, transfer to the oven and cook for 90 minutes, until lamb is fork tender. Discard lemon wedge.

    Serve with rice.

1½ lbs lamb shoulder, chopped

2 tsp sea salt

1 tsp ground black pepper

2 Tbsp + 1 tsp vegetable oil (divided)

1 white onion, finely chopped

2 tsp grated ginger

1 cinnamon stick

6 green cardamom pods

2 bay leaves

2 cloves garlic, finely chopped

½ tsp ground coriander

½ tsp ground cumin

½ tsp curry powder

½ tsp ground turmeric

¼ tsp cayenne pepper

¼ tsp fennel seeds

¼ tsp garam masala

1 c puréed tomatoes

½ red bell pepper, seeded, deveined and chopped

¼ lemon

1 Tbsp white vinegar

steamed rice, to serve

tomato-braised lamb shoulder and arugula pappardelle

pictured p. 152
serves 6

arugula pappardelle

6 c arugula

1 Tbsp extra-virgin olive oil

3 large eggs

1½ c Italian "00" flour, plus extra for dusting

1½ c semola flour

braised lamb shoulder

3 Tbsp vegetable oil

2 lbs boneless lamb shoulder, divided into 4 equal pieces

sea salt and ground black pepper

1 large onion, chopped

1 carrot, chopped

1 stalk celery, chopped

4 cloves garlic, chopped

2 c dry red wine

2 c canned crushed tomatoes

1 c Beef Stock (p. 201)

1 c Chicken Stock (p. 200)

¼ c maple syrup

2 Tbsp sherry vinegar

2 bay leaves

bunch of thyme

sprig of rosemary

continued facing

This is a winter dish that needs time, so get out the slow cooker, if you have one. After a few hours, the flavours meld and the lamb turns fork tender. You could add some potatoes to the dish if you'd like to make it a one-pot meal. Or serve with pasta, rice or any type of grain.

arugula pappardelle Fill a bowl with ice water. Set aside.

Bring a saucepan of salted water to a boil. Add arugula and blanch for 5 seconds. Transfer leaves to the ice bath to cool. Drain, then use your hands to wring out water from arugula. Roughly chop.

Combine arugula and oil in a food processor and process until coarsely mixed. With the motor still running, add eggs and process until arugula is finely chopped and eggs are mixed in. Set aside.

In a bowl, combine flours and mix well. Make a well in the centre, then pour in the arugula mixture. Mix together with a fork.

Transfer the dough to a lightly floured surface and use your hands to knead until the dough becomes smooth, silky and elastic. Wrap the dough in plastic wrap and set aside for 10 minutes before rolling or shaping.

To roll the pasta, lightly flour the work surface and the pasta machine. Set the rollers at the widest setting, then work a portion of the dough through the rollers. Fold the dough over itself and work through the rollers again. Repeat until the dough feels like suede.

Adjust the knob to the next narrowest setting and pass through the rollers again. Continue to pass the dough through the rollers, setting the machine down another notch after each roll. If the dough becomes too long to handle, cut it in half.

Roll the dough down to the last or second-to-last notch.

Transfer the pasta to a lightly floured work surface and cut into ½-inch-long strips. Set aside.

braised lamb shoulder Preheat oven to 350°F.

Heat oil in a large ovenproof frying pan over high heat, until nearly smoking. Season lamb with salt and pepper. Add lamb to pan and sear for 2 minutes, until browned on all sides. Transfer to a baking sheet.

Add onions, carrots, celery and garlic to the pan and cook for 5 minutes over medium heat, until tender. Pour in wine and bring to a boil, scraping any leftover bits of meat from the bottom of the pan. Cook for 10 minutes, until reduced by half.

Stir in tomatoes, beef and chicken stocks, maple syrup and vinegar. (The liquid should almost cover the lamb. If not, add more stock or water.) Bring to a boil and add bay leaves, thyme and rosemary. Cover tightly with a lid or aluminum foil and braise in the oven for 3 hours, or until the meat is fork tender. Set aside to cool, then refrigerate overnight to allow the flavours to develop.

The next day, remove the solidified fat from the surface. Heat the lamb over low heat until warmed through. Remove lamb, shred and set aside. Strain braising liquid and reserve for later.

assembly Bring a large pot of salted water to a boil. Add pappardelle and cook for 2 minutes. Drain and set aside.

Heat oil in a saucepan over medium heat. Add garlic and sauté for 1 minute, until garlic is tender. Add tomatoes and shredded lamb shoulder and sauté for 2 to 3 minutes. Pour in braising liquid and simmer for 10 minutes over low heat to develop flavour.

Add pappardelle, grated Parmesan and arugula and gently toss together. Taste and adjust seasoning if needed.

Serve with shaved Parmesan.

assembly

1 Tbsp olive oil

4 cloves garlic, finely chopped

24 grape tomatoes, halved

2 c reserved braising liquid

⅓ c grated Parmesan cheese, plus extra shaved Parmesan for garnish

3 c arugula

sea salt and ground black pepper, to taste

CHEF'S NOTE

To store the fresh-cut pasta, line a baking sheet with wax paper, add the pappardelle and place wax paper between each layer. Cover it with plastic wrap and refrigerate for up to 3 days.

**tomato-braised
lamb shoulder
and arugula
pappardelle**

p. 150

**seared venison
loin with white
bean–truffle
ragout**

p. 154

pictured p. 153
serves 4

seared venison loin with white bean—truffle ragout

marinated venison

2 cloves garlic, finely chopped

¼ c finely chopped sage

¼ c finely chopped rosemary

¼ c finely chopped Italian parsley

¼ c olive oil

¼ c sherry vinegar

1 lb venison striploin, cut into 4 steaks

ragout

2 c dried cannellini beans, soaked overnight

2 Roma tomatoes

½ Tbsp vegetable oil

3 oz double-smoked bacon, cut into a ¼-inch dice

1 shallot, finely chopped

2 cloves garlic, finely chopped

⅔ c dry white wine

⅔ c Chicken Stock (p. 200)

1 Tbsp Italian parsley, chopped

1 Tbsp unsalted butter

truffle oil, to taste

kosher salt and ground black pepper, to taste

continued facing

Venison is becoming more common because it's lower in fat than beef. And farmed or free-range venison isn't as likely to have the gamey taste of wild deer meat. Because it's so lean, the key to cooking venison is that it cannot go over medium-rare, or the meat becomes tough. We've paired it here with a decadent white bean ragout with truffle oil.

marinated venison In a bowl, combine all ingredients, except the venison, and mix well. Add venison and coat all sides in the marinade. Cover and refrigerate for 2 hours to marinate.

ragout Put beans in a saucepan of salted water and simmer for 30 minutes, or until beans are 90 per cent cooked. Drain, then set aside until needed.

Meanwhile, bring a small saucepan of water to a boil. Cut a small "×" into the bases of the tomatoes. Add to the pan and blanch for 30 seconds. Drain, then cool tomatoes under cold running water. Peel skin, then cut tomatoes in half and remove seeds. Chop and set aside.

Heat vegetable oil in a small saucepan over medium heat. Add bacon and sauté for 3 to 4 minutes. Add shallots and garlic and sauté for 2 to 3 minutes, until shallots are translucent. Pour in wine and cook for another 3 minutes, until reduced by half.

Add beans and stock and bring to a boil. Reduce heat to medium-low and simmer for 10 minutes, until beans are tender. Stir in parsley, butter, tomatoes and truffle oil. Season with salt and pepper. Keep warm.

morel sauce Soak morels in warm water for 10 minutes. Cut larger mushrooms in half. Drain, then shake off any excess water.

Heat oil in a frying pan over medium heat. Add mushrooms and shallots and sauté for 2 minutes. Pour in wine and deglaze pan for 1 minute. Increase heat to medium-high, then add stock and cook for 4 to 5 minutes, until liquid has reduced by three-quarters and is almost syrupy. Whisk in butter. Season with salt and pepper. Keep warm.

assembly Preheat oven to 400°F. Generously season venison with salt and pepper.

Heat oil in a large ovenproof frying pan over high heat. Add venison steaks and sear for 15 seconds per side, until browned on all sides. Place pan into the oven and roast for 3 to 4 minutes, until steaks are medium-rare. Transfer to a cutting board and set aside for 5 minutes to rest.

Spoon ragout into the centre of each plate, slice the venison and place on top. Spoon morel sauce around the ragout, garnish with chives and serve.

morel sauce

16 dried morels, stems trimmed
1 Tbsp vegetable oil
1 shallot, finely chopped
⅓ c dry red wine
⅓ c Chicken Stock (p. 200)
1 Tbsp unsalted butter, cold
kosher salt and ground black pepper, to taste

assembly

sea salt and ground black pepper
2 Tbsp vegetable oil
1 Tbsp sliced chives, for garnish

temperature chart for cooking meats

If you want to be certain of the doneness of your meat and not second-guess yourself, then invest in a good meat thermometer. Always approach the meat from the side as soon as it comes off the heat, inserting the thermometer horizontally into the thickest part of the cut, away from any bones that could throw off the reading. Push the tip of the thermometer as far into the flesh as possible, then slowly draw it out while watching the temperature reading. Some parts of the meat may produce higher readings than others, and that's okay. What you want is a cross-section of readings.

When the lowest reading you get is at the low end of the temperature range for your desired doneness, remove the meat from the heat completely. Set it aside for several minutes to rest, so the meat can relax and the residual heat can finish the cooking. Remember that the larger the cut, the more it will continue to cook while resting.

Type of Meat	Internal Temperature (°F)	Description
POULTRY		
Whole	Breast: 165; Thigh: 165–170	Insert the thermometer in the inner thigh, being careful not to touch the bone, and cook until the juices are clear
Parts	Breast: 165; Thigh: 165–170	
Stuffed	165	
Ground	170–175	
RED MEATS (BEEF, LAMB, DUCK, VENISON), STEAKS AND TENDERLOINS		
Rare	120–125	Slightly warm, bright red centre but pinkish toward the edges; soft to the touch
Medium-rare	130–135	Warm, very pink in the centre; slightly firm
Medium	140–145	Hot throughout, light pink in the centre; firmer to the touch
Medium-well	150–155	Hot throughout, mostly grey with a hint of pink in the centre; firm to the touch
Ground	160–165	
PORK		
Medium	140–145	Pale pink in the centre
Well done	160 and higher	Greyish brown throughout
Ground	160	

bison mushroom stroganoff
with thyme sour cream

serves 6

Here we go with another one-pot wonder. I used to work with a Swiss chef who added pickle juice to cut through the richness of his stroganoff. That simple trick was a game changer for me. Bison meat is beef's healthier cousin because it's lower in saturated fat, and quite common in a lot of butcher shops. But you can always sub out the bison with beef tenderloin or elk meat.

bison mushroom stroganoff Pat bison dry with paper towels and season with salt and pepper.

Heat oil in a large pan over high heat, until smoking. Add bison in a single layer and sauté for 2 minutes, until brown on all sides. Transfer to a baking sheet.

Melt butter in the same pan over medium-high heat. Add shallots and garlic and sauté for 1 minute, scraping up browned bits from the bottom of the pan. Add mushrooms and smoked paprika and cook for another 3 to 4 minutes.

Add cognac then pour in beef stock and simmer for 3 to 4 minutes, until liquid thickens and coats mushrooms. Stir in sour cream and mustard.

Add bison and any juices from the baking sheet and simmer over medium-low heat for 3 to 4 minutes, or until bison is heated through but still medium-rare. Stir in herbs. Season with salt and pepper.

Meanwhile, bring a large pot of salted water to a boil. Add noodles and cook for 8 minutes, or until tender. Drain noodles and transfer to the pan with the bison and sauce.

assembly Mix sour cream and thyme in a bowl. Transfer stroganoff to shallow bowls and serve with a healthy dollop of thyme sour cream on top.

bison mushroom stroganoff

1 (2-lb) bison loin, trimmed of silver skin, cut into 1-inch cubes

sea salt and ground black pepper

2 Tbsp vegetable oil

2 Tbsp unsalted butter

4 shallots, finely chopped

4 cloves garlic, finely chopped

1 lb button mushrooms, quartered

1 Tbsp smoked paprika

2 Tbsp cognac

1 c Beef Stock (p. 201)

¾ c sour cream

1 Tbsp Dijon mustard

1 Tbsp chopped thyme

1 Tbsp chopped Italian parsley

12 oz wide egg noodles

assembly

1 c sour cream

1 Tbsp chopped thyme

breads

flatbread

2 tsp instant yeast

4 c all-purpose flour, plus extra for dusting

2 tsp kosher salt

¼ cup extra-virgin olive oil, plus extra for brushing (divided)

Flatbread is a delicious all-purpose bread that is served throughout the Middle East. This version is super easy to make and requires no more than four ingredients, making it perfect to serve with a main dish like lamb and baba ganoush (p. 148) or even use as a base for pizza (p. 133).

In a medium bowl, combine yeast, flour and salt. In a separate bowl, mix 2 tablespoons oil and 1¾ cups water. Pour wet ingredients into dry and mix until a dough forms.

Transfer dough to a lightly floured work surface and knead until smooth. Grease the bottom and sides of a large bowl with the remaining tablespoon of oil. Add dough and turn to coat in oil. Cover with a dish towel and set in a warm place for 1 hour, until doubled in size.

Preheat grill over high heat to 400°F. Preheat oven to 425°F.

Gently press on the dough to release some of the air and transfer to a lightly floured work surface. Divide dough into 6 to 8 pieces and roll out into thin disks, about ⅛ inch thick. Brush the surfaces with oil.

Place flatbreads on the grill, oil-side down, and cook for 1 minute, until golden brown and lightly charred. Brush the tops of the flatbreads with more olive oil, turn over and grill for another minute, until golden brown. Transfer flatbreads to a baking sheet and bake for 5 minutes. Transfer to a plate and set aside until needed.

CHEF'S NOTE

If you'd like to make the dough in advance, simply mix it and then let it rise in the fridge overnight or for up to 48 hours. Cut the dough into 6 to 8 pieces and roll them out. Set aside until it's warmed to room temperature. Follow instructions for grilling and baking.

fruit and nut bread

This bread goes well with a foie gras appetizer because it's packed with fruit, which is a natural complement. Slice it thin and serve it with manchego cheese. Make this bread gluten free simply by replacing the all-purpose flour with a gluten-free version.

Preheat oven to 275°F. Line a 9- × 5-inch loaf pan with parchment and spray it lightly with oil.

In a large bowl, combine flour, sugar, salt, baking soda and baking powder and mix well. Add nuts and dried fruit and combine until mixture resembles granola.

In a separate bowl, combine eggs and vanilla and mix well. Add to the dry ingredients and stir in until the mixture nearly holds together. Pack into the loaf pan, evenly spreading it out into the corners. Bake for 40 minutes, or until golden brown and a toothpick inserted into the centre comes out clean.

Transfer bread to a cooling rack. Once cool, slice and serve.

2 c all-purpose or gluten-free flour

2 c packed dark brown sugar

2 tsp kosher salt

1 tsp baking soda

1 tsp baking powder

4½ c pecans, coarsely chopped

4½ c walnuts, roughly chopped

2 c dates, roughly chopped

2 c dried figs, roughly chopped

1½ c dried cranberries

1 c dried apricots, roughly chopped

10 large eggs

2 Tbsp vanilla paste

herb and garlic confit focaccia

Kat is the MacGyver of pastry chefs, and she will experiment late into the wee hours until she gets it right. She calls it "Dirty Apronizing." That means pulling from the classics and other cultures as well, merging flavours and techniques into sophisticated yet rustic dishes. A great example is this focaccia, for which garlic confit and its infused olive oil are added to a basic peasant bread. As a result, it's more cake-like and similar to brioche.

In a stand mixer fitted with the hook attachment, combine bread flour, semola flour, sugar, salt, yeast and 1¼ cups water. Mix on medium-low speed until dough is shaggy and barely holds together. Allow the dough to rest for 5 minutes. (During this resting stage, the flour absorbs the liquids that activate enzymes to develop gluten, and simple sugars start to form as the starch breaks down to feed the yeast. This process is known as autolyse.) Continue to mix on medium speed until dough comes together.

Slowly add garlic confit and oil and mix until emulsified and dough windowpanes when stretched. Add herbs and mix until just distributed.

Line a 9- × 13-inch pan with parchment paper and lightly oil. Place dough in the pan and set aside to rest for 5 minutes. Dimple the surface with your fingers and set aside for another 5 to 10 minutes. Continue to dimple the surface until the dough fills the entire pan. Cover pan with plastic wrap and refrigerate overnight.

Place pan in a warm area of your kitchen for 1 to 1½ hours, until dough has doubled in size. Lightly spray the surface with water and sprinkle with fleur de sel.

Preheat oven to 350°F.

Bake focaccia for 30 to 40 minutes, until golden and it reaches an internal temperature of 195°F to 200°F. Brush lightly with garlic confit olive oil as soon as it comes out of the oven.

3 c + 2 Tbsp bread flour

⅔ c semola flour

1 Tbsp granulated sugar

1½ tsp kosher salt

1 tsp instant yeast

½ c Garlic Confit (p. 198)

½ c Garlic Confit olive oil (p. 198), plus extra for brushing

3 Tbsp chopped herbs (such as rosemary, thyme, oregano and/or chives)

vegetable oil, for greasing

fleur de sel, for sprinkling

CHEF'S NOTE

Windowpaning is a way of checking that the gluten has properly formed and that your dough is emulsified. Once the dough starts to pull away from the sides of the bowl and make a slappy sound as you're mixing it, pinch off a fist-size piece. It should look shiny and feel silky smooth. Shape it into a rough rectangle, then, holding opposite sides of the rectangle in each hand, gently pull your hands apart to stretch the dough. Turn the dough 90° and stretch it again. Do this a few more times until you have a thin, translucent "windowpane." If your dough has not yet reached this stage, throw it back into the mixer and mix it for 2 minutes more.

tomato sesame brioche buns

poolish

⅓ c milk

⅓ c bread flour

2 Tbsp granulated sugar

1 tsp instant yeast

egg wash

2 egg yolks

pinch of salt

tomato sesame brioche buns

1 quantity Poolish (see here)

4 large eggs

2⅔ c bread flour

1 tsp kosher salt

¾ c + 2 Tbsp tomato paste

¾ c (1½ sticks) unsalted butter, cubed, at room temperature

vegetable oil, for greasing

Egg Wash (see here)

black and white sesame seeds, for topping

I often return from a trip with a photo of a bread or dessert that has inspired me, then ask our pastry chef to see what she can do. That's what happened when I came back from Spain. I imagined a beautiful tomato brioche, but with sesame seeds because I like the unconventional.

poolish Combine all ingredients in a bowl. Cover with plastic wrap and set aside in a warm area of the kitchen for 1 hour, or until dough has doubled in size. (Alternatively, place the bowl in the refrigerator overnight and take it out 30 minutes before you plan to mix the dough.)

egg wash In a small bowl, combine egg yolks, salt, and 2 tablespoons water. Mix, then strain to remove the chalaza and set aside.

tomato sesame brioche buns In a stand mixer fitted with a hook attachment, mix poolish, eggs, flour, salt and tomato paste on medium-low speed until the dough looks shaggy and barely holds together. Allow the dough to rest for 5 minutes. (During this resting stage, the flour absorbs the liquids that activate enzymes to develop gluten, and simple sugars start to form as the starch breaks down to feed the yeast. This process is known as autolyse.) Continue to mix on medium speed until dough comes together.

Add butter, cube by cube, and mix until butter is emulsified and the dough windowpanes when stretched (see Chef's Note on page 163).

Lightly coat a bowl with oil. Add dough ball, cover with plastic wrap and refrigerate overnight.

Line a baking sheet with parchment paper. Cut dough into 12 equal pieces and shape each piece into a round roll. Place rolls on the prepared baking sheet and cover with a wet dish towel. Set brioches aside to proof at room temperature for 1 to 1½ hours, until nearly doubled in size. Brush them with egg wash and sprinkle sesame seeds on top.

Preheat oven to 350°F.

Bake brioches for 25 to 30 minutes, or until a thermometer inserted into the centres reaches 190°F. Transfer to a wire rack to cool or serve hot from the oven.

charcoal brioche buns

makes 12

For visual appeal, this brioche is made black with activated charcoal, which is considered to have health benefits. In some cultures, it's added to food to filter toxins from the body and help with digestion. And in bread, it looks amazing. Activated charcoal can be found at health and vitamin stores and organic supermarkets.

poolish Combine all ingredients in a bowl. Cover with plastic wrap and set aside in a warm area of the kitchen for 1 hour, or until dough has doubled in size. (Alternatively, place the bowl in the refrigerator overnight and take it out 30 minutes before you plan to mix the dough.)

egg wash In a small bowl, combine egg yolks, salt, and 2 tablespoons water. Mix, then strain to remove the chalaza and set aside.

charcoal brioche buns In a stand mixer fitted with a hook attachment, combine poolish and eggs and mix at low speed. In a separate bowl, combine flour, charcoal and salt and whisk until well mixed. Slowly add the flour mixture to the bowl of the stand mixer and mix until the dough looks shaggy and barely holds together. (If desired, you can add black food colouring to make the dough darker.) Allow the dough to rest for 5 minutes. (During this resting stage, the flour absorbs the liquids that activate enzymes to develop gluten, and simple sugars start to form as the starch breaks down to feed the yeast. This process is known as autolyse.) Continue to mix on medium speed until dough comes together.

Add the butter, cube by cube, and mix until butter is emulsified and the dough windowpanes when stretched (see Chef's Note on page 163).

Lightly coat a bowl with oil. Add dough ball, cover with plastic wrap and refrigerate overnight.

Line a baking sheet with parchment paper. Cut dough into 12 equal pieces and shape each piece into a round roll. Place rolls on the prepared baking sheet and cover with a wet dish towel. Set brioches aside to proof at room temperature for 1 to 1½ hours, until nearly doubled in size. Brush them with egg wash.

Preheat oven to 350°F.

Bake brioches for 25 to 30 minutes, or until a thermometer inserted into the centres reads 190°F. Transfer to a wire rack to cool or serve hot from the oven.

poolish
½ c milk
½ c bread flour
1 Tbsp granulated sugar
1 tsp instant yeast

egg wash
2 egg yolks
pinch of salt

charcoal brioche buns
1 quantity Poolish (see here)
3 large eggs
2¾ c bread flour
¼ c activated charcoal powder
1 tsp kosher salt
black gel colouring (optional)
¾ c (1½ sticks) + 2 Tbsp unsalted butter, cubed, at room temperature
vegetable oil, for greasing
Egg Wash (see here)

developing flavour

When it comes to developing flavour in bread, we have a few tricks up our chefs' sleeves. Learn these basics, and you'll learn the difference between a middle-of-the-road loaf and a loaf of bread that's so good you've just got to eat the whole thing.

Good-quality bread is made with something called a pre-ferment, also known as a fermentation starter. Bakers use this starter to develop taste and texture: it gives it not only the flavour, but also the golden crust, well-structured crumb and great chew. In fact, it's nearly impossible to make tasty bread without it.

Experienced bakers always have a starter dough, which is a mixture of flour, water and wild or manufactured yeast that's been matured in a bucket somewhere in the kitchen. (Wild yeast is the naturally existing yeast found all around us, on vegetation such as plants, trees and fruit and even in the air, and it is essential to creating tangy sourdough breads as well as beers, wines and cheeses.) The starter is added to a new batch of dough not only to help it rise, but also to give it the maturity necessary to develop.

A good starter, which gives bread its character, is very much a product of its environment, and the quality of the flour, water and even the air can affect its taste. That's why San Francisco sourdough will taste different from a Vancouver sourdough.

At the Dirty Apron, our breads start with a variety of pre-ferments. Our brioche starts with poolish, a wet sponge you make one to twenty-four hours before you need it. The pâte fermentée is a classic French starter (nicknames include "chef" or "old dough") that we keep in a bucket for one to three days, but when well wrapped and airtight, it can be stored in the freezer for up to three months. We allow it to fully thaw for twelve to sixteen hours at room temperature prior to

use. The pâte fermentée starter also helps develop a nice crust on breads, which is why we use it for our mini country rolls (p. 168). But our most loved and coddled pre-ferment is our wild sourdough starter, which we affectionately refer to as "Helen." She is kept in the warmest area of our kitchen and is fed multiple times daily with a house blend of organic flours. Helen makes the most flavourful loaves with the best crust and crumb.

But using a pre-ferment isn't the only way to develop great flavour. Time is a factor, too. A long, slow, cold rise for dough is crucial in bread-making to develop crust, crumb and flavour. And your choice of leavening agent, and how it interacts with the flour, also affects taste. Yeast is a natural leavener, while baking soda and baking powder are chemical leaveners, and their reaction to simple sugars (when the flour's starch is broken down) will result in a different product. Baking soda and baking powder are alkaline powders that are activated by heat or acidity and give that rise in your baking. Acidic ingredients, such as yogurt or buttermilk, also give a flavourful tang. A quick bread, such as our buttermilk biscuit (p. 25), relies on baking soda as a leavening agent, which is activated in the recipe by the buttermilk to produce the carbon dioxide necessary to create those tall, buttery layers of goodness. If done right, they will stand straight and tall like soldiers. Our biscuit is inspired by puff pastry because instead of kneading the dough, you fold it over, manipulating it and developing those layers. Manipulation of the dough is yet another way to develop a dough's structure.

The other way to get that flavour into your bread recipes is to simply add herbs, spices, nuts, seeds, dried or fresh fruits, vegetables, syrups, citrus zest or garlic confit—the options are limitless.

country
rolls

p. 168

country rolls

pâte fermentée

1¼ c bread flour

½ c semola flour

½ c whole-wheat flour

¾ tsp kosher salt

½ tsp instant yeast

vegetable oil, for greasing

country rolls

1 quantity Pâte Fermentée (see here)

1½ c bread flour, plus extra for dusting

½ c semola flour

½ c whole-wheat flour

¾ tsp kosher salt

½ tsp instant yeast

These dinner rolls were the product of serendipity. When we first started the Dirty Apron, we had so little space that we couldn't even find a place to store a bucket of starter (p. 166), which is the pre-ferment that gives bread its terrific texture and flavour complexity as it ages. So our pastry chef made these rolls because the starter dough can be kept in a freezer instead.

pâte fermentée In a stand mixer fitted with a hook attachment, combine all ingredients and add 1½ cups water. Mix on low speed until it comes together. Increase to medium speed and mix until it becomes a rough dough.

Lightly coat a bowl with oil. Add dough ball, cover with plastic wrap and refrigerate overnight or for up to 3 days. (To freeze the dough for later use, remove from the refrigerator after one night and wrap it well in plastic wrap. Store in the freezer for up to 3 months. When you want to use it, simply thaw out and follow the rest of the instructions.)

country rolls Preheat oven to 350°F. Line 2 to 3 baking sheets with parchment paper.

Chop pâte fermentée into 1-inch cubes. Set aside until it reaches room temperature.

In a stand mixer fitted with a hook attachment, combine pâte fermentée and 1¾ cups water. Mix on low speed for 1 minute, until water turns milky and small pieces of pâte fermentée are distributed through the water (it won't be a homogenous mixture). Add flours, salt and yeast and mix until well combined and the dough windowpanes when stretched.

Lightly coat a bowl with oil. Add dough ball, cover with plastic wrap and set aside at room temperature for 1 to 1½ hours, until the dough has doubled in size.

Divide dough into 24 large or 48 small pieces. Shape them into footballs (bâtards) and set aside on the prepared baking sheets. Cover with plastic wrap and allow to proof at room temperature, until they are 1½ times their original size. (If you poke the dough and it remains indented, then it's ready for action.)

Dust with flour and lightly slash each piece lengthwise. (If you've under-proofed your dough, slash it deeper. If you've overproofed your dough, barely slash it.) Bake for 20 to 35 minutes, or to an internal temperature of 190°F. Transfer to a wire rack to cool or serve hot from the oven.

CHEF'S NOTE
Pre-shaped rolls can be frozen for later baking. Put the rolls on a baking sheet and freeze. Store them in large freezer bags and freeze for up to 3 months. When ready to use, set aside at room temperature to proof until they are 1½ times their original size. Slash the rolls lengthwise and bake for 20 to 25 minutes.

gluten-free naan bread

4 c + 2 Tbsp gluten-free flour
1½ Tbsp instant yeast
1 Tbsp kosher salt
1 Tbsp granulated sugar
2½ tsp powdered gelatin
2 large eggs
2 large egg whites
2 c milk
¼ c extra-virgin olive oil
1 Tbsp apple cider vinegar
ghee or canola oil, for frying and greasing

Many years ago, before the numerous commercial gluten-free flours and breads were on the market, Kat's son Caleb switched to a gluten-free diet, which could have been a challenge for a pastry chef. But she figured out ways to get around the wheat, and this naan is one of them. She also uses it double-duty as a pizza crust (p. 133) or as a flatbread base during our scholarship classes with the Canucks Autism Network, as it can easily be made vegan and even allergen-free with substitutions.

In a stand mixer fitted with a paddle attachment, combine all dry ingredients and mix on low. Slowly add wet ingredients and mix until well combined.

Divide dough into 4 equal pieces. Flatten each piece into an oblong shape on a 9- × 13-inch silicone mat or lightly oiled piece of parchment paper. (The final dimensions should fit into a 10-inch frying pan.) Cover each piece with lightly oiled plastic wrap and set aside to rise in a warm place for 1 to 1¼ hours, until the dough is slightly puffy. (This dough will NOT be double in size because it lacks gluten.) Remove plastic wrap.

Heat a tablespoon of ghee (or oil) in a 10-inch cast-iron frying pan over medium-high heat. With your hand on the underside of the mat or parchment paper, carefully and gently flip dough into the hot pan. Cook until brown, then flip and repeat for the other side. Transfer naan to a plate. Repeat with the remaining naan, adding more ghee (or oil) to the pan each time.

CHEF'S NOTE
To make a flavoured flatbread, add 1 teaspoon garlic powder and 2 tablespoons fresh chopped herbs after dry and wet ingredients have been mixed together.

make
it vegan

Replace milk with
non-dairy milk and
powdered gelatin
with granulated
agar-agar.

make it
allergen-free

1 Replace whole milk with non-dairy milk.

2 Substitute eggs/egg whites with either
of the following:

3 Tbsp ground flax **or** 3 Tbsp chia seeds
and 6 Tbsp water and 1 c water

Allow mixture to sit at least 15 minutes
and proceed with recipe.

3 Replace powdered gelatin with granulated
agar-agar.

desserts

makes 1 (9- × 13-inch) pan of bars

chocolate nourish bars

Kat created this dessert for my wife, Sara, who likes chocolate but wanted something healthy, too. It's gluten-free and vegan and packed with fibre, protein and omega-3s.

Preheat oven to 350°F. Line a baking sheet with parchment paper.

Add oats, almonds and pecans and toast for 8 to 12 minutes, stirring occasionally, until golden brown.

Bring a large saucepan of water to a simmer over medium heat. In a heatproof bowl, combine coconut oil, maple syrup, chocolate chips, almond butter, cocoa, vanilla and salt and place the bowl over the saucepan. Using a spatula, mix all the ingredients together until melted.

Remove bowl from heat and add toasted oats and nuts. Combine until they are well coated. Line a 9- × 13-inch pan with foil and then parchment paper and lightly coat with coconut oil. Pour in mixture and tap it down hard on the counter to even it out and to get rid of air bubbles. Refrigerate until mixture has set, but preferably overnight. Cut into rectangles and serve.

4 c quick oats

1⅔ c sliced almonds

1½ c roughly chopped pecans

2 c coconut oil, plus extra for greasing

1 c maple syrup

3½ c extra bittersweet (74%) chocolate chips

½ c almond butter

⅓ c cocoa powder

1 Tbsp vanilla paste

1 tsp kosher salt

vegan pumpkin-spice granola bars

pumpkin spice mix
¾ c ground cinnamon

2 Tbsp + 2 tsp ground ginger

2 Tbsp + 2 tsp ground nutmeg

2 Tbsp allspice

2 Tbsp ground cloves

granola bars
oil, for greasing

9 c quick oats

2½ c extra bittersweet (74%) chocolate chips

1½ c dried cranberries

3⅓ c dark brown sugar

1¾ c pumpkin purée

1 c maple syrup

2 Tbsp vanilla paste

1¼ tsp Pumpkin Spice Mix (see here)

1¼ tsp ground cinnamon

1¼ tsp ground nutmeg

1¼ tsp kosher salt

This bar was another creation that came about by chance. Due to a mistaken order, we ended up with too many cans of pumpkin purée, and we needed to use it quick because we didn't have the space to store it. This pumpkin bar was so versatile that it did duty for breakfast, as a snack and as a catering dessert. Now we're always ordering pumpkin.

pumpkin spice mix Combine all ingredients in an airtight container, close lid and thoroughly shake. Spice mix can be stored in an airtight container for up to 3 months.

granola bars Preheat oven to 325°F. Line a 12- × 16-inch baking sheet with parchment paper. Lightly oil the parchment.

In a large bowl, combine oats, chocolate chips and cranberries and mix well.

In a separate bowl, combine the remaining ingredients and mix well. Pour the wet mixture into the dry mixture and toss to evenly coat.

Tightly press mixture into the prepared pan. Bake for 20 minutes, or until bars are barely set and have not coloured.

Cut bars to your preferred size. Leftovers can be stored in an airtight container in the refrigerator for up to 1 week or for 3 months in the freezer.

makes 22 cookies # caramel macchiato cookies

For years, when we made up a batch of our famous fleur de sel caramels, we would have leftover bits of caramel, which the staff would gobble up. One day we had the realization that we could put those leftover bits to use, and this amazing cookie was born. The notes of coffee take it to another level. And don't feel bad for the staff: they still get lots of leftover bits from many other treats when they wander over to the pastry-making station.

browned butter Heat butter in a medium saucepan over medium-low heat. The butter will begin to separate, the top layer will begin to foam and the whey will float. Skim the whey and discard. You will be left with the milk proteins forming a crispy brown layer on the bottom of the pan and a clear light brown layer on top. Brown the crispy bottom layer as much as possible, without it turning black.

Place a piece of cheesecloth in a fine-mesh sieve and carefully strain the butter. Discard the crispy layer and reserve the liquid browned butter. (Makes 3 cups.)

Leftover browned butter (also known as *beurre noisette*) can be added to just about anything—it's gold.

caramel macchiato cookies Preheat oven to 350°F. Line a baking sheet with parchment paper.

In a stand mixer fitted with a paddle attachment, cream together browned butter and sugars. Add in vanilla paste and espresso coffee extract. Add eggs and egg yolks and mix well.

In a separate bowl, combine flour, cornstarch, baking soda and salt and mix well. Add dry ingredients to the wet ingredients and mix until a ball of dough forms. Stir in chocolate chips.

On a large piece of parchment paper, flatten cookie dough to a ½-inch thickness. Sprinkle instant coffee on top and roll like a Swiss roll, forming layers of dough and instant coffee. (Do not overmix, or you'll lose the speckled effect and the bursts of more intense coffee flavour in each bite.)

Scoop out ¼-cup dough balls and pat them into a 4-inch ring cutter. Set them on the prepared baking sheet. Place a salted caramel in the centre. Bake for 10 minutes, or until edges begin to brown.

browned butter

4 c (8 sticks) unsalted butter, cubed

caramel macchiato cookies

2 c Browned Butter (see here)
2 c packed dark brown sugar
1 c granulated sugar
2 tsp vanilla paste
2 tsp espresso coffee extract
3 large eggs
3 large egg yolks
5½ c all-purpose flour
½ c cornstarch
2½ Tbsp baking soda
2 tsp kosher salt
1¼ c milk chocolate chips
¼ c instant coffee crystals
22 Salted Caramels (p. 180)

Earl Grey lemon cookies

2½ c all-purpose flour

1 tsp baking soda

1 tsp baking powder

1 c (2 sticks) unsalted butter

1¼ c granulated sugar

2 tsp vanilla paste

3 egg yolks

1 heaping Tbsp Earl Grey tea leaves

coarse sugar, for coating

½ c fresh lemon juice, strained

½ c + 2 Tbsp confectioner's sugar

I wanted a tea-based cookie, and the best options were Earl Grey or chai. I preferred the former, because the tea's signature flavour is bergamot oil, which is extracted from the rind of a bergamot orange. Combined with lemon, it's a citrusy, lightly sweet union.

Preheat oven to 350°F. Line a baking sheet with parchment paper.

In a large bowl, combine flour, baking soda and baking powder.

In a separate bowl, cream butter, granulated sugar, vanilla paste and egg yolks. Add dry ingredients to the creamed mixture and mix until a ball of dough forms. (Do not overmix.)

In a stand mixer fitted with a paddle attachment, combine small portions of the dough and the tea leaves and pulse, until tea leaves are evenly distributed. Add more dough and tea leaves and keep pulsing. Repeat until all dough and tea leaves are used. (Again, do not overmix.)

Scoop out ¼-cup dough balls and pat into a 4-inch ring cutter. Roll in coarse sugar. Place on the prepared baking sheet and bake for 10 minutes, or until edges begin to brown.

Meanwhile, in a small bowl, combine lemon juice and confectioner's sugar. Brush lemon mixture on top of the hot cookies to form a glaze. Set aside to cool.

salted caramels

1 c (2 sticks) unsalted butter,
plus extra for greasing

3⅓ c packed dark brown sugar

1 (300-ml) can condensed milk

1 c dark corn syrup

1 Tbsp fleur de sel

1½ tsp vanilla paste

Customers come to our deli just for the caramels. They are such a bestseller that we wondered if we should even give out the recipe. But they're too good not to share. They are, hands down, the best salted caramels, ever.

Line an 8-inch square baking pan with parchment paper and lightly grease.

In a deep saucepan, combine butter, brown sugar, condensed milk and corn syrup and cook over medium-high heat until the temperature reaches 242°F on a candy thermometer. Stir with a spatula, to avoid burning the caramel. Remove from heat and stir in fleur de sel and vanilla paste.

Transfer mixture into the prepared pan and allow to cool. Cut into portions and wrap in wax paper.

serves 4   chia seed pudding

2 c coconut milk
½ c chia seeds
¼ c maple syrup
1 tsp vanilla paste
½ tsp ground cinnamon
½ tsp ground ginger
½ tsp ground cardamom
¼ tsp ground cloves
¼ tsp ground black pepper
3 c Raspberry Coulis (p. 183)
or raspberries

Loaded in omega-3, magnesium, calcium and fibre, chia seeds absorb a ton of fluid and create a gel-like consistency, which makes them a nutritious and unique foundation upon which to build flavour. You can also make this pudding using almond milk.

Mix all the ingredients, except for the raspberry coulis, in a bowl and transfer into an airtight container. Refrigerate for at least 30 minutes, or overnight.

Remove from refrigerator and layer parfait-style with raspberry coulis (or raspberries).

dark chocolate pâté

This pâté was created for our cooking school as part of our chocolate symphony trio plate. It's a chocoholic's fantasy come true: rich, smooth and totally satisfying. We use Valrhona's 64 per cent Manjari chocolate because of its fruity undertones.

dark chocolate pâté Melt dark chocolate in a double boiler (or in a bowl over a simmering pot of water). Stir in butter, until smooth. Remove from heat and set aside to cool to room temperature.

In a separate bowl, beat cream until soft peaks form. Using a spatula, fold cream into the cooled chocolate mixture.

Line a 9- × 5-inch loaf pan with plastic wrap. Spoon chocolate mixture into the pan, cover with plastic wrap and refrigerate for 2 hours.

raspberry coulis In a saucepan, combine raspberries and sugar and cook over low heat for 10 to 15 minutes, stirring occasionally. Strain through a fine-mesh sieve to remove seeds. Chill.

assembly Carefully remove the pâté from the loaf pan. Using a hot knife, slice the pâté and put onto dessert plates.

Serve with raspberry coulis, raspberries and toasted hazelnuts (or hazelnut praline).

dark chocolate pâté
2¾ c 64% to 74% dark chocolate chips
½ c (1 stick) unsalted butter
1⅓ c heavy (36%) cream

raspberry coulis
3 c fresh or frozen raspberries
½ c confectioner's sugar

assembly
fresh raspberries, for garnish
toasted hazelnuts or Hazelnut Praline (p. 186), for garnish

vegan avocado-almond-chocolate mousse

serves 4

You won't miss the dairy in this mousse! It tastes deliciously chocolatey and rich, but without the eggs and heavy cream. We usually use almond milk, but you can also use coconut, hemp or rice milk.

almond praline Process almonds in a food processor until coarse and mealy. Set aside.

In a small saucepan over high heat, combine sugar and 2 teaspoons water and allow mixture to caramelize until golden brown. (Do not stir.) Remove from heat and carefully fold in almonds until evenly distributed. Line a baking sheet with a silicone mat. Transfer mixture to it and set aside to cool completely.

Place mixture in a food processor and pulse until the praline is broken into small pieces.

avocado-almond-chocolate mousse Combine all ingredients in a food processor and mix until combined and smooth. Distribute mousse into 4 ramekins and garnish with almond praline.

almond praline
1 c toasted almonds
½ c granulated sugar

avocado-almond-chocolate mousse
1 ripe avocado
¼ c cocoa powder
¼ c maple syrup
¼ c almond milk
1 tsp vanilla paste

maple mascarpone cheesecakes

hazelnut praline

1 c toasted hazelnuts

½ c granulated sugar

maple mascarpone cheesecakes

1 c whipping (33%) cream

3 sheets gelatin

4 egg yolks

¼ c granulated sugar

⅓ c Marsala

⅓ c maple syrup

⅓ c mascarpone

1 c Hazelnut Praline, plus extra for garnish (see here)

1 cup assorted berries, for garnish

These no-bake cheesecakes take Marsala and maple zabaglione and up the richness with mascarpone. Be sure to make lots of extra praline because you can use it later to top off vanilla ice cream or plain Greek yogurt.

hazelnut praline Place hazelnuts in a food processor and process until coarse and mealy. Set aside.

In a small saucepan over high heat, combine sugar and 2 teaspoons water and allow mixture to caramelize until golden brown. (Do not stir.) Remove from heat and carefully fold in hazelnuts, until evenly distributed. Line a baking sheet with a silicone mat or greased parchment paper. Spread mixture onto it and set aside to cool completely.

Place mixture in a food processor and pulse until the praline is finely ground.

maple mascarpone cheesecakes In a medium bowl, whisk cream until soft peaks form. Set aside in the refrigerator.

In a small bowl, combine gelatin and 1 cup cold water and set aside for 5 minutes to bloom.

Fill a 2-litre saucepan a quarter full with water and bring to a simmer over medium-high heat. Reduce heat to maintain a constant low simmer.

In a medium heatproof bowl, combine yolks, sugar, Marsala and maple syrup. Place bowl over the pan of water and whisk until mixture is thick and foamy, and has reached 165°F on a candy thermometer. Remove from heat and whisk in the bloomed gelatin sheets, until dissolved and the mixture has cooled. Whisk in mascarpone, then gently fold in whipped cream and hazelnut praline.

Line the inside of four 3-inch ring molds with an acetate collar and wrap foil around the bottom of each mold so the contents cannot leak out. Place the molds on a baking sheet and pour in mixture. (Alternatively, line individual ramekins with plastic wrap, patting it flush against the ramekins. Pour in mixture.) Refrigerate for 3 to 4 hours. Carefully remove the cheesecakes from the molds (or ramekins), garnish with praline and berries and serve!

on a sweeter note

Let's be honest. When it comes to dessert, the words "gluten-free" and "vegan" don't excite most people. For many of us who remember the hippie vegetarian movement of the seventies, a lot of "healthy" desserts would use dry carob and had all the flavour of kibble. A recent *New Yorker* article was appropriately titled "How Carob Traumatized a Generation." I think I was one of them.

Well, those sad days are over.

Happily for pastry chefs, baking gluten-free or with plant-based ingredients has become easier due to the vastly wider variety of products available. As a result, we're seeing an explosion of gluten-free bakeries popping up in North American cities. We're also seeing gluten-free options on restaurant menus everywhere.

Professional cooks need to learn about these products and how to use them, because a substantial portion of the population has chosen to forgo gluten and animal products for health, ethical and environmental concerns. For example, eggs have always been an integral ingredient in baking, providing not just flavour, but moisture, binding and leavening. Now, there are a slew of highly nutritious alternatives, including ground flaxseeds, chia seeds or agar-agar (a substance made from seaweed or algae).

When choosing an egg substitute, our pastry chef Kat considers how the substitute will affect flavour and the final structure of the recipe. In recipes calling for egg whites, she uses aquafaba, the slightly thick water remaining after cooking chickpeas (or in a can of chickpeas). She makes both classic meringues and vegan gluten-free brioche from it, which sounds crazy, but the science works.

To add moisture in a recipe, we'll use vegetable or seed-based oils and nut butters, as well as fruit and vegetable purées. And of course, when it comes to vegan sweets, "Good-quality, dairy-free chocolate is your best friend," says Kat.

It's also not difficult to bake gluten-free—it just requires an understanding of the alternatives to wheat. Look to oats, nut flours, rice, buckwheat, cassava, amaranth, chia, flax, millet, quinoa, sorghum, tapioca and corn, and all the many other wheat-free products now readily available to bakers. You can easily grind your own flours and blend them to create different flavours. The tricky bit is that when baking without gluten, you need to figure out a way to give the dough its strength and elasticity. Gluten proteins, found in wheat, are the workhorses that trap the gases and create the airy structure that holds up a loaf of bread. Gluten-free bakers rely on gelatin, agar-agar, guar gums and xanthan gum to mimic gluten in doughs, giving the baked products their necessary structure. Others add carbonated water, ginger ale and beer to give their doughs that light and airy structure. In our kitchen, baking is a process of experimentation and elimination, to see what works.

Many of our Dirty Apron customers are on dairy-free and gluten-free diets, so we're fully on board with alternatives, including some of the recipes in this section. In fact, we would like these "alternatives" to become part of the norm and to lose their stigma, which they quickly are. Whether we're working with plant-based, gluten-free ingredients or otherwise, it always comes down to flavour.

fruit-filled
hand pies
p. 190

pictured p. 189
makes 8 small hand pies

fruit-filled hand pies

pastry dough
¾ c all-purpose flour, plus extra for dusting

¾ c pastry flour

¼ tsp kosher salt

¼ tsp baking powder

1 (3-oz) package cream cheese, cut into ½-inch cubes and frozen

½ c (1 stick) unsalted butter, cut into ½-inch cubes and frozen

2 tsp apple cider vinegar

blackberry filling
4 c blackberries

2½ Tbsp cornstarch

½ c granulated sugar

blueberry filling
4 c blueberries

2 Tbsp cornstarch

½ c granulated sugar

apple filling
4 c sliced Granny Smith apples

1 Tbsp cornstarch

¼ c granulated sugar

1 Tbsp ground cinnamon

continued facing

What's not to like about a deep-fried pie? The hand pie is a nod to the southern U.S. This pie dough is a Dirty Apron favourite because the dough has both butter and cream cheese, two fats that taste delicious and melt at different temperatures, creating a flavourful and distinctly textured crust.

pastry dough In a large bowl, combine flours, salt and baking powder.

In a food processor, combine a small portion of the cubed cream cheese and the flour mixture and pulse until the cream cheese cubes are a quarter of their original size. Repeat until all the cream cheese has been added, then repeat with the butter. Transfer mixture to a bowl.

In a small bowl, combine vinegar and 3 tablespoons ice water. Using your fingers, add vinegar mixture, a tablespoon at a time, to the flour mixture. The pastry dough should appear shaggy and barely hold together. Add a few more drops of ice water at a time, if needed. Do not knead.

Pat the dough into a flat disk and wrap it in plastic wrap. Refrigerate for at least 30 minutes or up to 24 hours. Or freeze the dough in this state for up to 3 months.

filling Choose your filling. In a large saucepan, combine all ingredients and set aside for 15 minutes to macerate, allowing the juices to come out of the fruit and until the sugar mixture looks like wet sand. (If needed, add up to 1 cup of water or juice.) Cook over medium heat for 8 to 12 minutes, until the fruit is softened and the mixture thickens and bubbles. Transfer to a bowl and chill.

glaze (optional) Melt butter in a saucepan over low heat, then add your preferred liquid and bring to a boil. Stir in sugar and vanilla paste. Keep warm and set aside.

assembly Heat oil in a deep fryer or deep saucepan to a temperature of 350°F. (Use a thermometer for an accurate reading.)

Lightly dust a work surface with flour. Roll out the dough to an ⅛-inch thickness and cut out 8 circles with a 4-inch cookie cutter. Add cold fruit filling to one half of each circle.

In a small bowl, combine egg yolks, salt and 2 tablespoons water. Brush egg wash on the perimeter of the circles and fold in half to create semi-circle pies. Using a fork, press along the edges to seal. (Alternatively, pleat the edges.)

Carefully lower the pies into the oil and deep-fry for 5 to 7 minutes, until both sides are golden brown. (Turn if needed.) Transfer pies to plate lined with paper towels.

Immediately roll pies in cinnamon sugar or dust with non-melting sugar and place them on a wire rack to cool. Alternatively, dip hot pies into warm glaze and allow to cool. Serve.

glaze (optional)
⅔ c (1⅓ sticks) unsalted butter
½ c water, coffee or citrus juice (such as lemon, lime, orange or yuzu)
4 c confectioner's sugar
1 Tbsp vanilla paste

assembly
canola oil, for deep-frying
all-purpose flour, for dusting
2 egg yolks
pinch of salt
cinnamon sugar, non-melting sugar or Glaze (see here)

serves 4   **tartes Tatin**

1 lb Classic Puff Pastry (p. 202)
1 c granulated sugar
½ c (1 stick)
4 Granny Smith apples
4 tsp ground cinnamon
vanilla ice cream, to serve

We teach this elevated French version of the American apple pie at our cooking school. Named after a hotel in the Loire Valley, this dessert is an ode to the culinary star of fall, which is the apple. Our version requires caramelization of Granny Smith apples before topping with pastry. Done right, the apple slices are overlapped in the sticky caramel yet keep their shape and texture.

Preheat oven to 400°F. Line a baking sheet with parchment paper.

Roll puff pastry out until ⅛ inch thick and cut 4 (5-inch) circles, using a circular cutter or a small plate as a template.

Place the disks on the prepared baking sheet, prick all over with a fork and refrigerate for 20 minutes.

In a heavy-bottomed saucepan over high heat, combine sugar and 2 tablespoons of water and cook until caramelized and golden brown. Carefully whisk in butter, then pour caramel evenly into 4- to 5-inch pie dishes and set aside to cool.

Peel, halve and core the apples. Thinly slice the apple halves crosswise.

Arrange apple slices in an overlapping circular shape around the base of each pie dish and dust with cinnamon. Cover each tart with a circle of puff pastry, ensuring all the apples are covered. Bake for 15 minutes, or until the pastry is cooked and crisp. Set aside tarts to rest for 5 minutes.

Carefully invert the tarts onto individual plates and top with scoops of ice cream.

olive oil and rosemary cake

½ c (1 stick) unsalted butter, room temperature, plus extra for greasing

1 c granulated sugar, plus extra for sprinkling

2 large eggs

6 Tbsp extra-virgin olive oil

4 tsp finely chopped rosemary

1½ c all-purpose flour

½ tsp baking powder

pinch of salt

ice cream, to serve

Rosemary is often overlooked in dessert-making, but its rustic, earthy notes pair wonderfully with this delicately sweet, simple cake. It's a touch savoury, for those of us who don't like our desserts too sweet.

Preheat oven to 325°F. Grease two 5- × 2½-inch loaf pans. Sprinkle sugar along the bottoms and give it a good shake. Tap out excess sugar (we just need it to coat the pan).

In a stand mixer fitted with a paddle attachment, cream together butter, sugar and eggs until light and fluffy. Slowly drizzle in oil and mix until emulsified. Using a spatula, fold in rosemary.

In a separate bowl, sift together flour, baking powder and salt and mix well. Gradually stir the dry ingredients into the wet ingredients. Pour batter into the prepared pans and spread evenly. Bake for 25 to 30 minutes, or until a toothpick inserted into the cakes comes out clean.

Set aside to cool in the pans for 10 minutes, then invert onto a wire rack to cool completely. Slice and serve with your favourite ice cream.

serves 4 caramel lemon semifreddo

Semifreddos are fantastic make-ahead frozen desserts for those who love the richness of ice cream and the smoothness of mousse, but do not own an ice cream machine. This recipe uses *pâte à bombe* (a sugar and egg base also used for mousse) to produce a light and fluffy semifreddo—and as an added bonus, it will hold its shape a little longer than other ice creams at room temperature.

caramel lemon semifreddo In a bowl, whisk egg yolks until thick and pale. Set aside.

In a separate bowl, whisk cream until stiff peaks form.

In a small saucepan, combine sugar and 2 teaspoons water and heat over medium-high heat, until the mixture just reaches the hard ball stage, which means a little of the syrup dropped in water will form a hard ball, or 247°F on a candy thermometer.

At this point, you must work quickly and safely. Slowly pour a steady stream of sugar syrup into the egg yolks, whisking continuously to fully incorporate. Whisk until the bowl has cooled down completely. Add lemon juice and zest and mix well.

Using a spatula, gently fold in whipped cream. The texture should remain light and fluffy. Spoon mixture into a container lined with plastic wrap. Freeze until firm.

praline dust In a small saucepan, stir together sugar and 2 teaspoons water and cook over medium-high heat until sugar turns a pale caramel colour. Remove from heat and set aside to let caramel darken to a deep brown.

Line a baking sheet with a silicone mat. Carefully pour mixture onto it and set aside to cool.

Using your hands, break praline into smaller pieces by hand. Using a mortar and pestle, grind praline into a fine dust.

assembly Slice semifreddo and place on dessert plates. Sprinkle praline dust overtop and serve.

caramel lemon semifreddo
4 egg yolks
1 c + 2 Tbsp heavy (36%) cream
6½ Tbsp granulated sugar
3 Tbsp fresh lemon juice
1 tsp grated lemon zest

praline dust
⅓ c granulated sugar
2 tsp water

basics

chickpeas

makes 4 cups

2 cups dried chickpeas
1 Tbsp salt

Place chickpeas in a large bowl, cover with water and soak overnight.

Drain chickpeas, then transfer them to a large saucepan. Cover with cold water, add salt and cook over medium heat for 1 hour, until soft but not falling apart. Drain and refrigerate until needed.

garlic confit

makes 2 cups

1 cup garlic cloves
1 cup extra-virgin olive oil

Preheat oven to 350°F.

In a small baking dish, combine garlic and oil and toss well. Cover with foil and bake for 30 minutes, or until garlic is tender. Uncover and bake for another 10 minutes, until garlic is very tender. Set aside to cool.

CHEF'S NOTE
Most recipes call for garlic confit, but the oil can be used as a separate ingredient as well.

pesto

makes 2 cups

4 c basil leaves
½ c extra-virgin olive oil
2 cloves garlic, finely chopped
¼ c pine nuts, toasted
⅓ c grated Parmesan cheese
kosher salt and ground black pepper, to taste

In a blender, combine basil, oil, garlic, pine nuts and Parmesan and purée until smooth. Season to taste with salt and pepper. Leftover pesto can be poured into ice cube trays and frozen for up to 1 month.

green curry paste

makes ¾ cup

8 green serrano chiles or jalapeños

6 kaffir lime leaves, torn

2 cloves garlic

1 stalk lemongrass, outer two layers discarded, finely chopped

1 shallot, chopped

1 bunch cilantro leaves, stems and roots

2 Tbsp chopped ginger

1 tsp peanut oil

1 tsp coriander seeds

½ tsp black peppercorns

¼ tsp kosher salt

grated zest of ½ lime

Combine all ingredients in a food processor and process into a thick paste. Transfer the paste to an airtight container. Leftover paste can be stored in the refrigerator for up to 3 weeks.

CHEF'S NOTE
With a distinctive aroma and herbal flavour, cilantro root is an essential Thai ingredient. They can be found in specialty Asian supermarkets or at local farmers' markets.

red curry paste

makes ¼ cup

12 small dried red chiles, seeded, soaked, drained and roughly chopped

½ shallot, chopped

1 clove garlic, chopped

3 white peppercorns

1 Tbsp chopped lemongrass

1 tsp coriander seeds

½ tsp chopped cilantro stems

½ tsp cumin seeds

½ tsp kosher salt

½ tsp shrimp paste

Put all ingredients in a food processor and blend to a thick paste. Transfer paste to an airtight container. The paste can be stored in the refrigerator for up to 3 weeks.

perfect pastes

You'll see recipes that include both red and green curry pastes in this book. Curry pastes are so versatile: they work as marinades and add flavour to sauces, aioli, soups and last-minute stir-fries. Try switching out the red curry for the green curry in the coconut duck soup (p. 73) or braised beef short ribs (p. 139). Or use the red curry in the chicken curry recipe. I encourage you to play around and see what different combinations you can come up with.

And best of all, curry pastes keep well in the freezer so you can prepare a large batch in advance and use it whenever you want.

vegetable stock

makes 6 cups

5 large carrots, finely chopped
2 stalks celery, finely chopped
1 large onion, finely chopped
½ bulb garlic
10 sprigs Italian parsley
5 sprigs thyme
10 white peppercorns
1 c white wine
1 c coriander seeds

Place all the ingredients in a large stockpot. Add 6 cups water, bring to a boil over medium heat and then simmer for 1 hour. Remove from the heat and allow to cool. Transfer the cooled stock to an airtight container and refrigerate overnight to allow the flavours to develop.

Strain the stock through a fine-mesh sieve into a large, clean bowl. Discard solids.

Stock can be stored in an airtight container and refrigerated for up to 5 days or frozen in small batches for up to 2 months.

chicken stock

makes 8 cups

bones from 2 to 3 chickens, chopped
and thoroughly rinsed
1 onion, skin on, coarsely chopped
2 stalks celery, coarsely chopped
1 large carrot, skin on, coarsely chopped
½ bulb garlic, halved
3 sprigs thyme
8 white peppercorns
2 bay leaves

Place all ingredients in a large stockpot. Pour in 8 cups water and bring to a boil over medium heat. Reduce the heat to low and simmer for 2½ hours, using a spoon to skim off any impurities that rise to the surface. Remove from the heat.

Strain stock through a fine-mesh sieve into a clean bowl. Discard solids. Stock can be stored in an airtight container in the refrigerator for up to 5 days or frozen in small batches for up to 2 months.

CHEF'S NOTE
Gently simmer, never boil stocks, as boiling will make the liquid go cloudy. Do not stir, either.

beef stock

makes 12 cups

11 lbs beef bones
3 Tbsp vegetable oil
2 onions, roughly chopped
3 carrots, unpeeled, roughly chopped
3 stalks celery, unpeeled, roughly chopped
1 bulb garlic, halved
6 sprigs thyme
15 whole black peppercorns
4 Tbsp tomato paste

Preheat the oven to 400°F. Place the beef bones in a roasting pan and roast until lightly browned, 1 to 1½ hours. Set aside.

Heat oil in a large stockpot over medium-high heat. Add onions, carrots, celery and garlic and sauté for 15 minutes, until caramelized. Stir in the thyme, peppercorns and tomato paste and cook for another 2 minutes. Add the beef bones, reserving the pan, and 6½ litres of water and bring to a simmer.

Place the roasting pan over high heat, add 2 cups of water and use a wooden spoon to gently release all the caramelized juices and pieces of meat stuck to the bottom of the pan. Pour this liquid into the stockpot. Simmer stock for 5 hours, skimming off any impurities that rise to the surface.

Strain the stock through a fine-mesh sieve set over a large, clean saucepan. Discard solids. Bring to a boil, reduce heat to medium and simmer until it is reduced to 3 litres (about 1 hour). Remove from the heat and set aside to cool.

Stock can be stored in an airtight container for up to 5 days or frozen in small batches for up to 2 months.

pizza dough

makes 1/2 lb

½ tsp active dry yeast
1 c Italian "00" flour, plus extra for dusting
1 tsp kosher salt
1 tsp granulated sugar
2 tsp extra-virgin olive oil

In a small bowl, combine yeast and ⅓ cup lukewarm water and set aside for 5 minutes.

In a medium bowl, combine flour, salt and sugar. Using your hands, create a small well in the centre and pour in the yeast mixture. Using a fork, stir it into the dry ingredients until it becomes too difficult to mix. Use your hands to mix the dough until it pulls away from the sides of the bowl.

Transfer the dough to a lightly floured work surface and knead until it is smooth but remains slightly sticky. Dust the surface with extra flour if needed.

Place dough in a small bowl and add a drizzle of oil, ensuring dough is evenly coated to prevent sticking. Cover with plastic wrap and allow to proof for 1 hour, or until doubled in size. Dough can be used right away or frozen for later use.

classic puff pastry

makes 1 lb

1 tsp fresh lemon juice or white vinegar
½ tsp kosher salt
3 Tbsp unsalted butter, melted
1⅓ c + ¼ c all-purpose flour (divided)
½ c pastry flour
1 c (2 sticks) unsalted butter, room temperature

Use this traditional method when you have the time.

Combine ½ cup ice water, lemon juice (or vinegar) and salt in a bowl and mix until the salt is dissolved. Stir in the melted butter.

Place the 1⅓ cups of all-purpose flour and the pastry flour in a bowl and mix well to combine. Pour the flours into a mound on a clean work surface and make a well in the centre. Pour three-quarters of the liquid into the centre of the well. Working from the centre outward, use your fingers to draw small amounts of the flour into the liquid. Keep working in the flour this way until it becomes a paste and then a thick and shaggy dough.

Using a bench scraper or a bowl scraper, cut the dough into smaller pieces, lifting it and folding it as you go. You want to expose as many wet surfaces as possible to evenly incorporate the remaining flour. (Add more liquid, a few drops at a time, only if the dough appears too dry.) The dough should be shaggy, not too sticky and without any signs of dry flour. Shape the dough into a 5-inch disk, wrap it tightly in plastic wrap and refrigerate for at least 1 hour.

While the dough is resting, place the butter and the ¼ cup of all-purpose flour in a bowl and knead with your hands or a mixer until the flour is evenly distributed throughout the butter. Shape this butter into a 4-inch square, wrap tightly in parchment paper and refrigerate for at least 30 minutes.

1. Lightly dust a clean work surface with flour. Remove the dough and the butter from the fridge and make sure they are the same level of firmness. (If the butter is too soft, refrigerate it a bit longer. If it is too firm, leave it on the counter to soften to the same firmness as the dough.) Roll the dough into a 7-inch circle. Place the square of butter in the centre.

2. Using a bench scraper (or a sharp knife), lightly trace the outline of the butter on the dough, then remove the butter and set it aside.

Rolling outward from each side of the outlined square (but not touching it), gently stretch out the dough until you have 4 "flaps," each 3 to 3½ inches long.

3. Unwrap the butter and place it on the dough, then fold each flap partway over the butter. Do not overlap the flaps of dough; their edges should just meet at a spot in the middle of the butter.

4. Press the edges of the dough together to create a tight seal over the butter. Using a rolling pin and applying even pressure, gently pound the dough section by section until it is 1 inch thick. (Doing this will make the dough malleable and easier to roll. The dough should be cool and flexible, but not soft. If it is too soft, refrigerate it until it is cool. If it is hard, allow it to warm slightly. You want dough that will not crack the butter when it is rolled.)

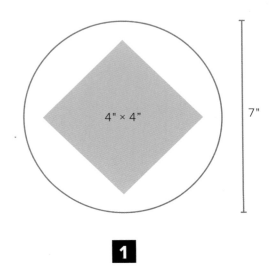

1

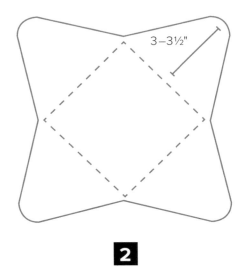

3–3½"

2

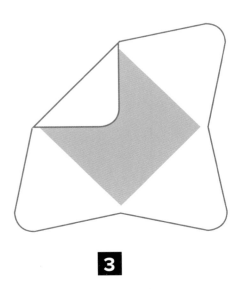

3

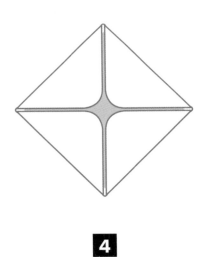

4

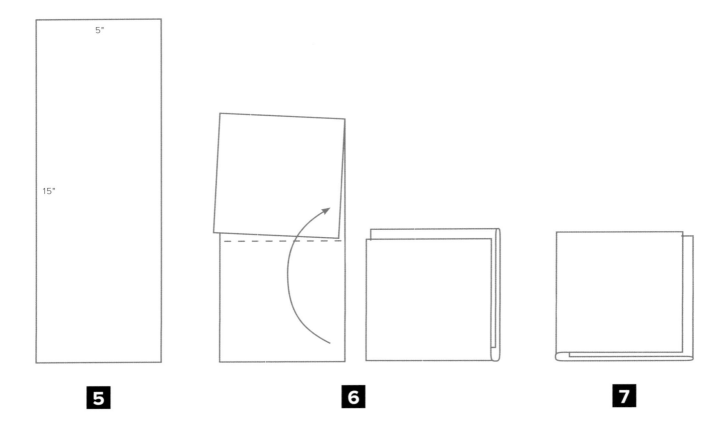

5

6

7

5. Rolling: Lightly dust a clean work surface with flour. Gently roll out the dough to a 5- × 15-inch rectangle, lifting it and adding more flour underneath from time to time to ensure that it does not stick. Brush off all excess flour.

6. Folding: Arrange the rectangle with the short side parallel to the counter edge. Fold the top third of the dough down and the bottom third of the dough up, as if you were folding a letter.

7. Turning: Ensure the edges of the dough are lined up neatly and all the corners are square. Turn the dough 90 degrees so the open sides are parallel to the counter.

This process of **rolling**, **folding** and **turning** is called a **single turn**. Once you have completed this single turn, dust the pastry with flour and wrap it in plastic wrap. Refrigerate for a minimum of 30 minutes or up to 24 hours.

Unwrap the pastry, and repeat the process of five more single turns. Allow to rest in the refrigerator for a minimum of 1 hour or up to 24 hours. The dough is now ready to use. Or freeze the dough in this state for up to 3 months.

rough puff pastry

makes 1 lb

1 tsp fresh lemon juice or white vinegar
½ tsp kosher salt
1½ c all-purpose flour
1 c (2 sticks) unsalted butter, cut into
½-inch cubes and frozen

Use this version when you're in a hurry.

Combine ½ cup ice water, lemon juice (or vinegar) and salt in a small bowl and stir until the salt is dissolved. Set aside.

In a food processor with an S-shaped blade attachment, pulse the flour and butter in batches until the butter cubes are half their original size. Transfer mixture to a large bowl.

Pour wet mixture into the large bowl and mix well with your hands, until dough looks shaggy and barely holds together. (Add more cold water if needed.) Do not knead the dough—the larger the butter piece, the flakier the pastry will be.

Lightly dust a clean work surface with flour. Set the dough on the counter and pat it into a 5-inch square. Roll the dough into a 5- × 15-inch rectangle, lifting the dough and adding more flour underneath, as necessary, to prevent it from sticking. Brush off all excess flour.

Arrange the rectangle with the short side parallel to the counter edge. Fold the bottom third of the dough up and the top third of the dough down, as if you were folding a letter. Ensure the edges of the dough are lined up neatly and all the corners are square. Turn the dough 90 degrees so the open sides are parallel to the counter. This process of rolling, folding and turning is called a single turn. Repeat this process for three more single turns. Dust the pastry block with flour and wrap it in plastic wrap. Refrigerate for 1 hour.

Unwrap the pastry, and repeat the folding for two more single turns. Allow to rest in the refrigerator for a minimum of 1 hour or up to 24 hours. The dough is now ready to use. Or freeze the dough in this state for up to 3 months.

CHEF'S NOTE
You can cut the pastry into individual portions before freezing it. Be sure to use a very sharp knife and cut straight down. Don't use any sawing or circular motions, as these will seal and crush the layers you've been working hard to create.

metric
conversion chart

weight

IMPERIAL	METRIC
½ oz	15 g
1 oz	30 g
2 oz	60 g
3 oz	85 g
4 oz (¼ lb)	115 g
5 oz	140 g
6 oz	170 g
7 oz	200 g
8 oz (½ lb)	225 g
9 oz	255 g
10 oz	285 g
11 oz	310 g
12 oz (¾ lb)	340 g
13 oz	370 g
14 oz	400 g
15 oz	425 g
16 oz (1 lb)	450 g
1¼ lbs	570 g
1½ lbs	670 g
2 lbs	900 g
3 lbs	1.4 kg
4 lbs	1.8 kg
5 lbs	2.3 kg
6 lbs	2.7 kg

liquid measures
(for alcohol)

IMPERIAL	METRIC
1 fl oz	30 ml
2 fl oz	60 ml
3 fl oz	90 ml
4 fl oz	120 ml

cans and jars

IMPERIAL	METRIC
14 oz	398 ml
28 oz	796 ml

volume

IMPERIAL	METRIC
⅛ tsp	0.5 ml
¼ tsp	1 ml
½ tsp	2.5 ml
¾ tsp	4 ml
1 tsp	5 ml
½ Tbsp	8 ml
1 Tbsp	15 ml
1½ Tbsp	23 ml
2 Tbsp	30 ml
¼ c	60 ml
⅓ c	80 ml
½ c	125 ml
⅔ c	165 ml
¾ c	185 ml
1 c	250 ml
1¼ c	310 ml
1⅓ c	330 ml
1½ c	375 ml
1⅔ c	415 ml
1¾ c	435 ml
2 c	500 ml
2¼ c	560 ml
2⅓ c	580 ml
2½ c	625 ml
2¾ c	690 ml
3 c	750 ml
4 c/1 qt	1 L
5 c	1.25 L
6 c	1.5 L
7 c	1.75 L
8 c/2 qts	2 L

linear

IMPERIAL	METRIC
⅛ inch	3 mm
¼ inch	6 mm
½ inch	12 mm
¾ inch	2 cm
1 inch	2.5 cm
1¼ inches	3 cm
1½ inches	3.5 cm
1¾ inches	4.5 cm
2 inches	5 cm
2½ inches	6.5 cm
3 inches	7.5 cm
4 inches	10 cm
5 inches	12.5 cm
6 inches	15 cm
7 inches	18 cm
8 inches	20 cm
9 inches	23 cm
10 inches	25 cm
11 inches	28 cm
12 inches (1 foot)	30 cm
13 inches	33 cm
18 inches	46 cm

temperature

(for oven temperatures, see chart at right)

IMPERIAL	METRIC
90°F	32°C
120°F	49°C
125°F	52°C
130°F	54°C
135°F	57°C
140°F	60°C
145°F	63°C
150°F	66°C
155°F	68°C
160°F	71°C
165°F	74°C
170°F	77°C
175°F	80°C
180°F	82°C
185°F	85°C
190°F	88°C
195°F	91°C
200°F	93°C
225°F	107°C
250°F	121°C
275°F	135°C
300°F	149°C
325°F	163°C
350°F	177°C
360°F	182°C
375°F	191°C

oven temperature

IMPERIAL	METRIC
200°F	95°C
250°F	120°C
275°F	135°C
300°F	150°C
325°F	160°C
350°F	180°C
375°F	190°C
400°F	200°C
425°F	220°C
450°F	230°C

baking pans

IMPERIAL	METRIC
5- × 9-inch loaf pan	2 L loaf pan
9- × 13-inch cake pan	4 L cake pan
13- × 18-inch baking sheet	33 × 46 cm baking sheet

acknowledgements

My heartfelt gratitude goes out to all of the incredibly talented and hard-working people who helped make our second Dirty Apron cookbook a possibility.

I am so grateful to all our friends and family who've supported, encouraged and believed in us over this last decade (even when a few others told us we were crazy to open a business at the time that we did).

It's so important to me to acknowledge the Dirty Apron staff who continue to help us create a place of excellence and inspiration. You've elevated our workplace to a place of love, respect and belonging. You have all become an extended family to my own sweet family. Thank you for your hard work, for your perseverance and dedication, and for keeping our customers happy—day in, day out.

A huge thank-you to Figure 1 Publishing for helping us put together yet another fantastic cookbook. Your hard work put *The Dirty Apron Cookbook* on the map—and it continues to generate buzz. We know this second book is going to deliver again, thanks to your talented team.

A special thank-you goes out to Kerry Gold, who helped me write this book. It's a highlight to work together again. Thank you for capturing my voice so authentically—you've knocked it out of the park!

Kevin Clark, you made my dishes come alive with your incredible photographs. You truly went above and beyond my expectations. I am so grateful for all the extra time you invested in making this book so visually stunning. Bravo, my friend.

And my deep gratitude to God, for giving us this special experience that is the Dirty Apron, and for allowing us to take our blessings and pay them forward to help others.

Every year, thousands of vulnerable men, women and children are traded and exploited around the world, including Canada. Human trafficking is a form of modern-day slavery and its abolishment is a cause that is very dear to our hearts. The Dirty Apron will donate $1 from the sale of every copy of this book to the Joy Smith Foundation, an incredibly important organization that is dedicated to the elimination of human trafficking in Canada by supporting the rehabilitation of human trafficking survivors and implementing prevention and awareness strategies to keep families safe. To learn more about the Joy Smith Foundation and the work it does, visit www.joysmithfoundation.com.

index

about the author

David Robertson began his career at age fifteen as a dishwasher in a restaurant kitchen—and thirty years later, he hasn't looked back. Since founding The Dirty Apron Cooking School and Delicatessen, he teaches more than thirty-five classes to 8,000 students each year. He found his passion when cooking for others, and he's extremely pleased that he so inspired one of his daughters that she too wants to be a chef. In his off-time, David likes to cook for kids in Vancouver's Downtown Eastside and fundraise for his favourite charities. He and his wife and business partner, Sara, believe we can break down the barriers between people with the art of good food. He is also the author of *The Dirty Apron Cookbook*.